Spike Lee's "Do the Right Thing" brings together essays that analyze this controversial film from a variety of perspectives. Among the topics examined are the production history of the film, the use of music, and the urban sociology of New York in the 1980s. Collectively the essays connect the interracial strife of New York as treated in *Do the Right Thing* with the contemporary social climate of and racism in the United States. The volume also includes reviews of the film by influential critics, a selection of production stills, a filmography, and a select bibliography.

Spike Lee's *Do the Right Thing*

CAMBRIDGE FILM HANDBOOKS SERIES

General Editor

Andrew Horton, *Loyola University, New Orleans*

Each CAMBRIDGE FILM HANDBOOK contains essays by leading film scholars and critics that focus on a single film from a variety of theoretical, critical, and contextual perspectives. This "prism" approach is designed to give students and general readers valuable background and insight into the cinematic, artistic, cultural, and sociopolitical importance of selected films. It is also intended to help readers grasp the nature of critical and theoretical discourse on cinema as an art form, a visual medium, and a cultural product. Filmographies and select bibliographies are included to aid readers in their own exploration of the film under consideration.

Spike Lee's
Do the Right Thing

Edited by

MARK A. REID

CAMBRIDGE
UNIVERSITY PRESS

PUBLISHED BY THE PRESS SYNDICATE OF THE UNIVERSITY OF CAMBRIDGE
The Pitt Building, Trumpington Street, Cambridge CB2 1RP, United Kingdom

CAMBRIDGE UNIVERSITY PRESS
The Edinburgh Building, Cambridge CB2 2RU, United Kingdom
40 West 20th Street, New York, NY 10011-4211, USA
10 Stamford Road, Oakleigh, Melbourne 3166, Australia

© Cambridge University Press 1997

First published 1997

Printed in the United States of America

Typeset in Stone Serif

Library of Congress Cataloging-in-Publication Data
Spike Lee's *Do the Right Thing* / edited by Mark A. Reid.
p.   cm. – (Cambridge film handbooks series)
Filmography: p.
Includes bibliographical references.
ISBN 0-521-55076-9 (hardcover). – ISBN 0-521-55954-5 (pbk.)
1. Lee, Spike.   2. *Do the Right Thing* (Motion picture)   I. Reid,
Mark (Mark A.)   II. Series.
PN1997.D63S65   1997
791.43'72 – dc20   96-36604
                                                       CIP

A catalog record for this book is available from
the British Library.

ISBN 0-521-55076-9 hardback
ISBN 0-521-55954-5 paperback

Photo credits
Figure 14: © 1986, Island Pictures. All rights reserved.
Figures 1, 4, 5, 6, 7, 8, 9, 10, 11, 12, 13, 17, 18, 19 20, and 21: © 1989,
    Universal Studios, Inc. All rights reserved.
Figures 15 and 16: © 1990, Universal Studios, Inc. All rights reserved.
Figures 2 and 3: © 1994, Universal Studios, Inc. All rights reserved.

*For artists, activists, and
intellectuals who use their skills to
dismantle oppressive systems*

Contents

Contributors

William Grant, ABD, is a doctoral candidate in the Radio, Television and Film Program at Northwestern University. He is also a filmmaker.

Victoria E. Johnson, ABD, is a doctoral candidate in the Critical Studies Program at the University of Southern California. Her essays have appeared in several film-related journals.

Douglas Kellner is Professor of Philosophy at the University of Texas, Austin. His publications include "Brecht's Marxist Aesthetics: The Korch Connection," in *Bertolt Brecht: Political Theory and Literary Practice*, Betty Weber and Herbert Heinen, eds. (University of Georgia Press, 1981), and (with Michael Ryan) *Camera Politica: The Politics and Ideology of Contemporary Hollywood Film* (Indiana University Press, 1988). He is a founder of one of the most important experimental cable television groups in the Southwest. Kellner is a renowned Marxist scholar as well as an accomplished videographer.

W. J. T. Mitchell is the Gaylord Donnelley Distinguished Service Professor in the Department of English Language and Literature and the Department of Art at the University of Chicago. He is editor of the journal *Critical Inquiry* and author of several books, including *Picture Theory* (University of Chicago Press, 1994).

Catherine Pouzoulet is Associate Professor of American Studies at the University Charles de Gaulle–Lille III in France. She is one of the leading young political scientists studying New York City racial and ethnic politics. She has written a book-length manuscript on the African-American experience in the politics of New York City and has published several articles on race relations there.

Mark A. Reid is Associate Professor of English and Film Studies at the University of Florida, Gainesville, where he teaches African-American literature, black diasporic cultural studies, and film. Reid is a coeditor of *Le cinéma noir americain* (CinemAction, 1988) and the author of *Redefining Black Film* (University of California Press, 1993) and *PostNegritude Visual and Literary Culture* (SUNY Press, 1997). His essays appear in Mbye Cham's *Exiles: Essays on Caribbean Cinema* (Africa World Press, 1992), Barry Grant's *Film Genre Reader II* (University of Texas Press, 1995), and Michael T. Martin's *Cinemas of the Black Diaspora* (Wayne State University Press, 1995).

Acknowledgments

I would like to thank the *Boston Globe,* the *Chicago Tribune,* and the *New York Times* for granting me permission to reprint the film reviews. I also wish to acknowledge the university presses of California and Chicago for reprint rights for the Victoria Johnson and W. J. T. Mitchell essays, respectively.

There are many people whose friendship and scholarship helped me while I gathered and edited the materials included in this volume, and I would like to mention a few of them. Jacqui Etheridge of BFI Stills, Posters and Designs and Terry Geesken of the Museum of Modern Art stills collection helped me select most of the film stills that illustrate this volume. I benefited immensely from the intellectual support and friendship of my colleagues at the University of California, Davis: Carl Jorgensen, Jacob Olupona, David Van Leer, and Clarence Walker, as well as my friends Kuan-Hsing Chen, Naifei Ding, Steve Look, Sergio Mims, Scott Simmon, Shoggy Waryn, and John Williams. Sylvie Blum freely offered her editorial skills and has been a great intellectual and spiritual resource. My undergraduate students at both the University of Florida, Gainesville, and the University of California, Davis, provided the stimulus that forced me to reconsider my previous criticisms of Spike Lee's *Do the Right*

Thing; the essays included in this book reflect my reappraisal of the film.

During the two years that I spent editing this film handbook, the Dean's Office of the College of Letters and Science and the English Department at the University of California, Davis, provided me with the necessary equipment and travel funding to finish my work. I thank the university faculty, staff, and administrators for their support.

Andrew Horton, the series editor, Beatrice Rehl and Lisa Stollar, the Cambridge University Press media studies team, and Mary Racine, my production editor, have my sincere appreciation.

MARK A. REID

Introduction

THE FILMS OF SHELTON J. LEE

On March 27, 1957, in Atlanta, Georgia, Shelton J. Lee (A.K.A. Spike Lee) was born to Jacquelyn, a schoolteacher, and Bill, a jazz composer-musician. During Lee's infancy, his family moved to New York City and resided in the integrated Brooklyn neighborhoods of Crown Heights, Cobble Hill, and Fort Greene, where he attended P.S. 294, Rothschild Junior High. In a few of his feature films, Lee uses his intimate knowledge of these racially integrated Brooklyn neighborhoods to dramatize the sometimes violent encounters that occur between African-Americans and their nonblack New York City neighbors.

Like many middle-class African-American children who grew up in the 1960s, Spike Lee was raised on popular culture that included movies featuring James Bond and the Beatles. Lee reminisces, "I can remember my mother, Jacquelyn, taking me to see James Bond movies. She liked them. I used to like old 007 myself. I remember seeing *Help!* with the Beatles and *A Hard Day's Night.*"[1] Lee and his siblings had many opportunities to learn to appreciate other art forms as well. His mother shared her interest in the performing and visual arts with her children. Their frequent family outings to films and plays would later influence the children's career choices. Lee states:

I

My mother was always taking me places to see the performing arts. I was grounded in the arts. I can remember so clearly how she took me to the Radio City Music Hall . . . to see *Bye Bye Birdie*. I also remember her taking me to Broadway to see *The King and I* with Yul Brynner when I was four or five years old. . . . All this exposure started my interest in the visual arts. My siblings and I were exposed to the arts, all of 'em. This happened as soon as we could walk. I believe exposure makes all the difference in the long run.[2]

Spike Lee's familial loyalty helped launch the artistic careers of his sister, Joie, and his two brothers, Cinque and David. Lee has also helped publicize the musical talents of his father, Bill Lee. He gave his siblings and father opportunities to work on major studio productions. Consequently, David was given a rare opportunity to join the National Association of Broadcast Employees and Technicians.[3] Lee employed several members of his family when he shot his first feature, *She's Gotta Have It* (Island Pictures, 1986). He gave Joie an acting credit, Cinque a production assistant credit, and David a still cinematographer credit; Bill Lee wrote the original music score. In Lee's second feature, *School Daze* (Columbia, 1988), Joie had a more prominent acting role, Cinque was an apprentice editor, and David was a still cinematographer. Spike employed Bill Lee to write the original score for his New York University student films, *Sarah* (1981) and *Joe's Bed-Stuy Barbershop: We Cut Heads* (1982);[4] Bill also scored the music for *School Daze* and the Universal Pictures *Do the Right Thing* (1989),[5] *Mo' Better Blues* (1990), and *Jungle Fever* (1991).

From 1975 to 1979, Lee attended his father's alma mater, Morehouse College, a historic black college in Atlanta whose alumni include Dr. Martin Luther King, Jr. Lee graduated from Morehouse with a bachelor of arts degree in mass communications. The following summer, he interned with Columbia Studios and entered New York University's Film School in the fall. While studying at NYU, he cultivated a working friendship with a fellow film student, cinematographer Ernest Dickerson. In recalling his NYU years with Dickerson, Lee says:

> Ernest and I were in the same class. We came in together. He was from Howard. I was from Morehouse. . . . We were the only blacks at NYU. There were two sections the first year and we were in different sections. The second year he shot my film *Sarah.*
>
> In my senior year he shot *Joe's.*[6]

In 1981, with Dickerson behind the camera, Lee made his master of fine arts thesis film, *Joe's Bed-Stuy Barbershop: We Cut Heads. Joe's* won the Best Student Film Award from the Academy of Motion Pictures Arts and Sciences. It was the first student film ever shown at Lincoln Center's "New Directors, New Films" series. The Academy Award and Lincoln Center screening brought Lee's talent to the attention of film executives, critics, and the general public. Lee established his production company, Forty Acres and a Mule Filmworks, and employed Ernest Dickerson as the cinematographer for most of the features produced by the company.

Lee's reputation grew with the favorable reception of his first feature-length film, *She's Gotta Have It,* at the 1986 San Francisco Film Festival. Luckily, Island Pictures saw the film and contracted to distribute it. Island Pictures took it to the Cannes Film Festival, where it received the 1986 Prix de Jeunesse–Best New Director. The Spike Lee and Ernest Dickerson filmmaking team brought continued artistic success to films made by Forty Acres and a Mule Filmworks.

In 1988, Lee memorialized his Morehouse College experiences in *School Daze.* This film presents an interesting image of black fraternity and sorority life; some scenes portray fraternity and sorority rivalry that explodes into musical numbers. The confrontations that occur between radical students and conservative college administrators resemble what happens between adventurous adolescents and their anxious parents. This particular film and other Forty Acres and a Mule Filmworks presentations exhibit a distinct appreciation of family-like loyalty. First and foremost, Lee is interested in his biological family, and dutifully includes them in the making of his films. In addition, his films portray a brotherly attachment to neighborhood types who form an extended black family.

THE EXTENDED FAMILY AS BLACK COMMUNITY

She's Gotta Have It, DRT, Mo' Better Blues, and *Crooklyn* (Universal, 1994) feature characters whose democratic ambitions are challenged by harsh social realities. In *She's Gotta Have It,* a young black woman named Nola wants to maintain a steady sexual relationship with three different men. In *DRT,* Buggin' Out, a politicized black teenager, demands that an Italian-American pizzeria owner place photographs of black personalities alongside the images of Italian-American celebrities that adorn the pizzeria's wall. Buggin' Out argues that since blacks patronize the pizzeria, images of black celebrities should be included on the wall. These two films explore philosophical issues that impinge on the economic. Nola and Buggin' Out disagree with generally accepted social conventions – monogamy and private property rights. Economic issues are dealt with more directly in the other two films, in which individuals are pawns in the marketing strategies of the entertainment industry.

In *Mo' Better Blues,* Bleek, a jazz musician-composer, never controls the financial aspects of his artistic labors. In *Crooklyn,* Woody Carmichael, the father of five children and an unemployed jazz musician-composer, refuses to compose and perform mainstream jazz music. Woody never takes a job to help Carolyn, his schoolteacher wife, feed their five children. *Crooklyn* and *Mo' Better Blues* pay tribute to the inventive art of black jazz musicians while dismissing their ability to reap monetary rewards from their work. Both films criticize the American entertainment industry, which, according to the films, selectively

FIGURE I
Buggin' Out (Giancarlo Esposito) incites a rebellion against Sal's Famous Pizzeria. (From the editor's collection.)

markets jazz by catering to the taste of the largest segment of the *paying* public. Nonetheless, Woody is partially at fault for his stubborn refusal to find work outside of the industry that destroys him and his family.

The four films portray Nola, Buggin' Out, Bleek, and Woody as pawns of either social conventions or the entertainment industry. Socioeconomic forces flatten dreams and diminish the hopes of each of the four characters, who threaten the status quo.

The success of Nola's polygamous heterosexual relationships with three black men would prevent a conventional marriage to one man and submission to his paternal authority. The "maintenance men of family values" want to know which of these men will marry Nola. Lee subtly indicts these merchants of nineteenth-century morality in an age of single parenthood, AIDS, and planned parenthood. *She's Gotta Have It* attempts to show how monogamy can oppress a woman like Nola. *DRT* dramatizes a situation in which a pizzeria owner's racial insensitivity leads to the death of a young black man. Unlike the events in *DRT*, those portrayed in *Mo' Better Blues* and *Crooklyn* do not lead to the death of their male characters. *Crooklyn,* however, ends with the death of Carolyn, the hardworking mother of five. The film does not criticize nineteenth-century sexual conventions that oppress libertine women like Nola; it does, however, criticize a father's capricious actions and show how his frivolity contributes to his wife's untimely death. In addition, the film shows Troy, a ten-year-old girl, performing her deceased mother's household duties because her father has not changed his ways.

Both *Mo' Better Blues* and *Crooklyn,* to various degrees, depict

FIGURE 2
Troy Carmichael (Zelda Harris), the ten-year-old daughter of Carolyn Carmichael (Alfre Woodard), learns responsibility from her mother in *Crooklyn*. (From the editor's collection.)

FIGURE 3
Troy learns poetry from her father, Woody Carmichael (Delroy Lindo), in *Crooklyn*. (From the editor's collection.)

the entertainment industry's exploitation of black jazz musicians and composers, who, out of economic necessity, are forced either to perform and compose music for the largest listening public or to live unproductive lives. Unlike Lee's subtle criticism of sexism in *She's Gotta Have It,* the films *DRT, Mo' Better Blues,* and *Crooklyn* present chilling images of black oppression by brutal police and an exploitive entertainment industry. Spike Lee creates populist hero(ine)s and films them within a black culturalist philosophical frame.[7]

Lee's films tend to honor a defeated African-American as populist hero(ine). In American film, this sort of character was prominent in such Frank Capra social comedies as *Mr. Deeds Goes to Town* (Columbia, 1936) and *Mr. Smith Goes to Washington* (Columbia, 1939). In these two Depression era films, the Anglo-American hero is oblivious to the machinations of big business and the existence of political corruption; the hero puts up a good fight but never changes the system. In like manner, Lee's films show the unceasing hope yet waning possibilities of a spirited African-American hero(ine) whose success requires a constant fight against systemic racism and, in Nola's case, sexism. Lee's protagonists find themselves caught in choke holds that suffocate opportunities, destroy democratic dreams, and pull hero and heroine into a self-destructive bitterness. These individuals are far from the mountaintop dreamt by Dr. Martin Luther King. Lee is trying to show his multiracial audience that many African-Americans are increasingly rejecting Dr. King's nonviolent tactics as a means to achieve social and economic equality in the United States.

These films in general, and *DRT* in particular, dramatize a static African-American geographical location in which neighborhood personalities infuse the film with a 1960s version of the black community. In *DRT* these figures include a friendly alcoholic (Ossie Davis as Da Mayor), a wise black matron (Ruby Dee as Mother Sister), nonblack shopkeepers (Danny Aiello, as Sal, and the Korean grocer), and policemen. If there is drug use, it consists in the consumption of alcohol, the inhaling of glue, and the smoking of marijuana. These *unthreatening* images occur in some of Lee's films (with the exception of contemporary images of crack cocaine use in *Jungle Fever* and *Clockers*).

A SYNOPSIS OF *DRT*

Do the Right Thing presents the destructive results of a meltdown, on the hottest day of the year, of interracial and interethnic civility between people who share one block in the Brooklyn neighborhood of Bedford-Stuyvesant. Sal, the Italian-American owner of Sal's Famous Pizzeria, has been selling pizza in this Bedford-Stuyvesant neighborhood for twenty years. He employs his two sons, Pino (John Turturro) and Vito (Richard Edson), and the African-American pizza delivery man, Mookie (Spike Lee). Sal and his sons do not live in this predominantly black neighborhood. Mookie, on the other hand, lives in the neighborhood and most of its African-American and Puerto Rican residents respect him. Mookie is the mediating character who tries to ease the racial animosity between Sal and two black teenagers, Buggin' Out and Radio Raheem.

Buggin' Out (Giancarlo Esposito) is a pseudo–black nationalist who sports an African pendant around his neck but still wears stylish white, unlaced Air Jordan basketball shoes. His fashionable urban dress defuses his political statements: he is so full of himself and his hip-hop look that his politics appear comical.

For instance, Buggin' Out enters Sal's to buy a slice of pizza and, as he begins to eat, becomes increasingly bothered by the photographs of Italian-American personalities who decorate the "Wall of Fame" in Sal's pizzeria. He asks Sal why he doesn't include some photographs of African-American personalities, since Blacks constitute a large part of Sal's clientele. Sal callously replies, "You want brothers up on the Wall of Fame, you open up your own business, then you can do what you wanna do. My pizzeria, Italian Americans up on the wall."[8] Buggin' Out will not accept Sal's slight. He thoughtfully responds, "Sal, that might be fine, you own this, but rarely do I see any Italian Americans eating in here. All I've ever seen is Black folks. So since we spend much money here, we do have some say."[9] Sal and Buggin Out's verbal altercation develops into Buggin' Out's efforts to organize a boycott of Sal's Famous Pizzeria.

In the next scene featuring Buggin' Out, Clifton (John Savage), a white yuppie who owns a brownstone on the block, accidentally bumps into Buggin' Out and steps on his Air Jordans, which elicits a moderately heated exchange. Buggin' Out's bombastic performance is lost on Clifton, who coolly proceeds into his flat.

Buggin' Out's physical threats are windy and his threatened boycott never materializes because the neighborhood residents see through his sham. Radio Raheem (Bill Nunn), however, is quite a different character: after Sal has two violent encounters with him, the black communities coalesce in a spontaneous assault on Sal's Famous Pizzeria.

Radio Raheem is a respected and feared teenager who carries a large portable radio blasting rap music. In one scene he intimidates Puerto Rican youths sitting on a stoop listening to salsa. In another, he verbally assaults a Korean shopkeeper, who nervously searches for the correct batteries for Radio's radio. Now, with his radio blasting "Fight the Power," Raheem enters Sal's Famous Pizzeria. Unlike the others, Sal isn't flustered by Radio Raheem's muscular build, belligerent demands, and wailing radio, and he sternly tells Radio to turn the music off. Radio grudgingly complies and receives a slice of pizza. On another occasion, however, Sal and Radio Raheem have a similar verbal exchange that turns into a physical wrestling match. The New York City police arrive and one officer places a choke hold on Raheem, who suffocates. The black community, angered by Raheem's senseless death, directs its rage at Sal's pizzeria. Racism as personified by both Radio Raheem's death and Sal's racial insensitivity becomes the match which ignites the torch that destroys the pizzeria.

DRT vividly portrays how a twenty-four-hour period can erupt into a seething interracial and interethnic display of mistrust that will further explode into civil disobedience and, in the "real world," into urban uprisings that leave many dead or homeless.

THE IMPORTANCE OF *DRT*

DRT received an Academy Award nomination for best original screenplay and the Best Director and Best Picture Awards from the Los Angeles Film Critics Association. The film is Lee's first serious dramatization of New York's current racial problems. It is, as the essays in this volume argue, the U.S. film industry's most serious treatment of contemporary forms of racism, which Lee subsequently developed in *Jungle Fever*. In *Jungle Fever*, Lee continues his treatment of New York's racial problems and dramatizes the love–hate relationship he and other black New Yorkers have with their Italian-American neighbors. Lee reminds his audience, initially in *DRT* and then in *Jungle Fever*, that people cannot be contained by the imagined raciogeographical spaces of white Bensonhurst or black Harlem.

The two films dramatize the unwanted, immoral and disloyal interaction between the Italian- and African-Americans through characters like *DRT*'s Sal, who works in a black Brooklyn neighborhood, and *Jungle Fever*'s Flipper and Angie, who meet somewhere between black Harlem and white Bensonhurst for a brief love affair. Both films generally portray urban America's ongoing racial fights between the nonblack working classes and African-Americans and, in particular, reflect New York City's hostile social climate.

Nevertheless, *DRT* advances Lee's creative vision of the black community as his extended family. It is a populist version of a black community – in this case a single block in a predominantly black Bed-Stuy neighborhood – in which there still exist brotherly sharing and civil interaction between black people. This fictional community is seasoned with Puerto Rican stoop sitters, a WASP brownstone owner, an Italian-American pizzeria owner and his two sons, a Korean-American couple, and a very significant "We Love Radio 108 FM" African-American disc jockey. The interaction occurs among diverse races, ethnic groups, and social classes, regardless of the fact that it appears unwanted or racially disloyal. This film will remain an important fixture in the American film canon because Lee weaves a complex image of the inescapable social exchanges that occur in an increasingly diverse America.

THE ESSAYS

The essays in this anthology use various critical strategies to interpret the cultural importance of Lee's film as both a political and an aesthetic statement about African-American life and experiences. I have selected these particular essays because they do not always agree with my earlier criticisms of *DRT*. They represent the diverse critical opinions that continue to attract popular and scholarly interest in *DRT* and the artistry of Spike Lee. Some authors analyze how the film dramatizes racial hostility between lower-class black urbanites and nonblack merchants who have businesses in the black community but live elsewhere. Other authors extend their analysis of *DRT*'s dramatization of racial hostility to consider how artists use, and have used, politics to create public art.

William Grant, in "Reflecting the Times: *Do the Right Thing* Revisited," traces the pre- and postproduction history and the popular and mainstream critical reception of *DRT*. He argues that Lee welcomed the controversy that his film attracted; and some critics have even suggested that he willfully sought and manipulated the media coverage. He also discusses the general absence of black members in the lily-white film trade unions. These unions are one of the last production-oriented areas of Hollywood that retain the vestiges of Hollywood's racist past. Presently, the film trade and technical unions determine if and when blacks are hired as crew members on any film regardless of who directs, produces, or stars. In exploring these inequities, Grant discusses how a predominance of white film technicians affects the production process, and how Lee placed more people of color in the trade unions' rank-and-file membership. The essay explores the relevance of both cultural and economic issues to black empowerment in the American film industry.

In "The Cinema of Spike Lee: Images of a Mosaic City," Catherine Pouzoulet, an urban sociologist, argues that the Los Angeles uprising following the Rodney King–Simi Valley jury decision gave new relevance to the political message of *DRT*. Whereas Lee's Brooklyn ghetto is romanticized for aesthetic purposes, Pouzoulet finds that Lee has carefully selected didactic images to present a vision of New York City's politics and the evolution of black community empowerment that resulted from the post–civil rights rearrangement of preexisting residential demographics of black middle, working, and lower classes in northern urban communities.

Victoria E. Johnson's "Polyphony and Cultural Expression:

Interpreting Musical Traditions in *Do the Right Thing*" discusses the film's music score and employs theoretical principles to analyze the film's musical construction of an African-American, northern urban folk culture that is centered on the auditory qualities of this specific culture.

According to Douglas Kellner, Spike Lee has emerged as one of today's most prolific, successful, and controversial filmmakers. In "Aesthetics, Ethics, and Politics in the Films of Spike Lee," Kellner interrogates Lee's narrative politics by a comparative reading of Lee's *DRT, Malcolm X* (Warner Brothers, 1992), and his other films. Kellner argues that Lee's aesthetics are Brechtian, while his politics integrate modern and postmodern positions that reflect Lee's black culturalist identity politics. Moreover, Kellner argues that it is undetermined whether *DRT* is a modernist text in search of a politics of black liberation or a postmodern deconstruction of modern politics. If one reads the text as a search for a (modern) political morality and politics of liberation, it is undecidable whether Lee privileges Malcolm X or Dr. Martin Luther King, or produces an open modernist text that forces the reader to think through the work. Kellner develops a reading of Lee's *Malcolm X* to see what light the film sheds on Lee's politics and aesthetic strategies, as well as the tensions and ambiguities in his cinematic production.

In "The Violence of Public Art: *Do the Right Thing*," W. J. T. Mitchell discusses the film as representative of public art in an age when distinctions between violence and its visual simulation have been morally obscured. He argues that the relevant context for *DRT* is its immediate situation in the summer of 1989, a historical moment in which the relation between public symbols, media images, and works of public art seemed to reach an especially intense focus in widely circulated spectacles of violence. To list some of the notable events in mass media and public culture in the late 1980s is to sense a new relation between visual images, violence, and the public sphere: the fall of the Berlin Wall and the icons of Soviet socialism; the televising of the Tiananmen Square massacre and the destruction of the

Goddess of Democracy; the controversy over desecration of the American flag and the circulation of new racial stereotypes in the American mass media; the controversies over works of art that seem to present a violent affront to public taste (Serra's "Tilted Arc"; Serrano's "Piss Christ"; Mapplethorpe's photographs of black sadomasochistic sexual practices). Mitchell asserts that *DRT* makes sense if one views the film as a comment on violence and public spectacle. He argues that the film is a cinematic critique of the violence of public images. Mitchell finds that *DRT* intervenes in an increasingly polarized and difficult situation for African-Americans as both subjects and objects of public visual display and systemic violence.

The essays included here indicate the various ways one can teach and study film, the performing arts, and cultural studies. Scholars, students, and film buffs alike will appreciate the way in which each of the essays traces the historical importance of *DRT*. Readers will also learn how Spike Lee imaginatively used a mainstream film to criticize the Koch mayoral administration. More important, readers will discover that Lee thwarted the racist efforts of the predominantly white New York film technical and trade unions, which tried to stop Lee from hiring black nonunion crew members, even though these same unions lacked a sufficient number of black union members to supply Lee with an adequate film crew.

NOTES

1. Spike Lee with Ralph Wiley, *By Any Means Necessary: The Trials and Tribulations of the Making of "Malcolm X"* (New York: Hyperion, 1992), p. 2.
2. Ibid.
3. Spike Lee with Lisa Jones, *Do the Right Thing: A Spike Lee Joint* (New York: Simon & Schuster, 1989). Lee writes that *Do the Right Thing* was his first union film (p. 107).
4. Spike Lee with Lisa Jones, *Uplift the Race: The Construction of "School Daze"* (New York: Simon & Schuster, 1988), p. 333.
5. Henceforth, referred to as *DRT*.

6. Spike Lee & Lisa Jones, *Spike Lee's Gotta Have It: Inside Guerrilla Film-making* (New York: Simon & Schuster, 1987), pp. 32–33.

7. In Chapter 4, Douglas Kellner argues that "Lee presents racism in personal and individualist terms as hostility among members of different groups, thus failing to illuminate the causes and structures of racism." I agree with Kellner's observation and will add one comment. Lee's black nationalism is posited by Buggin' Out, who resembles the type of populist white heroes found in Frank Capra films. Lee's populism, however, features a black individual caught in the claws of white industry and institutions and, in the case of Nola, patriarchal conventions.

8. Lee with Jones, *Do the Right Thing*, p. 141.

9. Ibid., p. 142.

I **Reflecting the Times**

DO THE RIGHT THING REVISITED

Huey Newton was slain
and we all felt the pain
of Yusef Hawkins
(Sadat X, Brand Nubian, 1990)

It has been almost ten years since *Do the Right Thing* (*DRT*) was released, yet its impact on the revolution in black cinema is still being felt. Spike Lee's successful track record has prompted Hollywood studios to invest in a host of low-budget black films that they expect will yield high profits. *House Party* (1990), *Boyz N the Hood* (1991), *New Jack City* (1991), *Menace II Society* (1993), and *Friday* (1995), to mention only a few, are the beneficiaries of Lee's success. An industry that has historically suppressed, diminished, and caricatured Blacks is now suddenly willing to take a chance on African-American filmmakers when their films are financially successful.

Lee has been able to change the course of black film by making respectable profits, although he has received meager capital investment from studios. This clearly illustrates that the struggle over film representation is determined mainly by economic factors and the interests of multinational corporations rather than by the concerns of filmmakers. However, if a particular studio believes that a film project can be packaged in such a way as to guarantee large profits for investors, disagreements over content are negotiable.

A look at the film industry's portrayals of African-Americans before *DRT* is instructive. In such films as *Cry Freedom* (1987), *Mississippi Burning* (1988), and *Glory* (1990), the African-American struggle is a subtext for white heroism. For example, in *Cry Freedom,* a film that purportedly portrays the well-known black South African antiapartheid activist Steve Biko, a white journalist is the central character. Consequently, Biko's anti-apartheid struggle is completely overshadowed.

Conversely, in *DRT,* African-Americans and their experience are the major focus. The sights and sounds of black America erupt into a cataclysmic denouement produced partially by circumstance and partially by the characters' own agency. Many studios were reluctant to invest money in Lee's project because of its inflammatory nature. Lee was finally able to secure the financing for *DRT* through a negative pickup deal, which required the studio to buy the rights to distribute his film before it was made. Still, theater owners and film critics feared that the film would ignite the flames of racial violence. Critic David Denby had this to say: "If Spike Lee is a commercial opportunist, he's also playing with dynamite in an urban playground. The response could get away from him."[1] Luckily, Universal and many theaters chose to ignore such fears. In the final analysis, *DRT*'s popular reception caused many to view the film as a valid commentary on the African-American urban experience.

This essay chronicles Spike Lee's battle to maintain his artistic integrity while making *DRT.* It describes his struggles with the studio and New York trade unions and is based largely on the production notebook in the companion volume to the film. Moreover, in describing Lee's experience of shooting *DRT,* this essay indicates how African-American visual artists struggle for control of the imaginative representation of African-American life and experience.

PLEASE BABY, PLEASE BABY

"I'll be one happy fool to see us have our own business right
here. Yes, sir. I'd be the first in line to spend the little money I
got."

(ML [Paul Benjamin] in *DRT*)

Film production begins not with the camera but with the
checkbook. As with the financing of any other Hollywood film,
DRT's production budget had to be guaranteed by the film company that would distribute the finished product. *DRT* presented
several challenges to the standard formula for distribution by a
major studio. Unlike a typical blockbuster, it featured no famous
stars. Its subject matter was unconventional by Hollywood stan-
dards. But it did have Spike Lee, a successful director with a
proven track record. Lee's first feature, *She's Gotta Have It* (1986),
cost just $175,000 to produce and earned close to $8 million.
School Daze (1988) came in at a cost of approximately $6.5 mil-
lion[2] and had domestic box-office sales of $14 million.

The merchandising of *DRT*, as with Lee's two earlier films, was
to be handled by his production company, Forty Acres and a
Mule Filmworks. There had been companion volumes to the
earlier films – *Spike Lee's Gotta Have It* and *Uplift the Race: The
Construction of "School Daze"* – and widespread marketing via T-
shirts, sound tracks, buttons, letter jackets, and baseball caps.
Lee's comment, "Somebody wearing your T-shirt is a walking
billboard,"[3] explains the strategy of placing his films' names and
the Forty Acres logo on a variety of merchandise.

Because of its subject matter, *DRT* represented a major shift
from Lee's two previous feature films. The film was not a modern
romance like *She's Gotta Have It*, with three men vying for the
affections of Nola Darling. Nor was it a black version of a college
musical like *School Daze*. *DRT* was a sobering and somewhat
frightening journey into the seething cauldron of inner-city pathology and racial tension. Were American audiences ready to
visit a black neighborhood and confront its inhabitants on their

own terms? Lee insisted that the set be located in the heart of Bedford-Stuyvesant. He balked at the presence of New York City police, who might, Lee believed, turn the Bed-Stuy block into an armed camp.

As the preproduction phase bidding began, Paramount and Touchstone were Lee's top choices for studios, with his primary choice being Ned Tannen's Paramount Pictures. Lee mused that since Paramount Communications owned the Knicks, "I might get the season tickets to the games I need and deserve. Regardless, I'm looking for a home, where I can make the films I want to make without outside or inside interference."[4] Even though Lee's two earlier films were made at Island and Columbia, respectively, he did not consider either studio the one for *DRT*. Island Pictures had fallen by the wayside even before *School Daze* because it lacked the necessary financial resources.

In considering Columbia Pictures, Lee reported that working with David Puttnam and David Picker was "ideal." When Dawn Steel took over production at Columbia, Lee writes, "we both went at it from the start. I don't like her taste, don't like her movies" (*DRT*, p. 31). Lee knew that more than a strained relationship was involved. "The importance of promotion was driven home when *School Daze* was released in February 1988. It had the misfortune to come out when Columbia was changing leadership, which resulted in the firing of the team of David Puttnam and David Picker. The new team, Lee has said, 'left his film to die.' "[5] He took personally the failure of the new studio chief, Dawn Steel, and Columbia Pictures to promote *School Daze* adequately. It was apparent he would not seek financing from Columbia. As his brief relationship with Columbia Pictures came to an end, Lee said:

> The classic nightmare of a filmmaker has happened to me, I'm caught in a regime change. Dawn Steel and her crew don't give a fuck about *School Daze* or any film that was made under Puttnam. They can say what they wanna say, but I know better. Their actions prove it. (*DRT*, p. 57)

Obviously, no love was lost between Spike Lee and Dawn Steel. After the misguided marketing of *School Daze*, it made sense for Lee to look for a new studio. Eventually he took control over the publicity for his film by finding support on black college campuses and universities, an effort that may well have saved the film from oblivion. Not only did *School Daze* receive a better-than-average box-office return of $14 million based on its cost of $5.8 million, but it was one of the few profitable films distributed by Columbia Pictures during the Picker–Puttnam reign at Columbia.

For *DRT*, Lee first negotiated with Paramount Pictures. As a result of his experience making *School Daze*, his first studio film, he knew that he would demand a contractual agreement that would give him the right to approve the final cut, a privilege extended to few directors. *School Daze* was financed via a negative pickup deal. Columbia was required to buy the rights to distribute the film and the money was then used to produce the film. Several films have been produced in this way, and the primary benefit to the director is the right to approve the final cut. Of course there are alternatives. For instance, a screenplay can be sold to the studio and remain at the studio's mercy, or the studio can finance the production and the filmmaker then loses artistic control.

What transpired during negotiations over *DRT* is an excellent example of Lee's tenacity and artistic integrity. His initial pitch to Paramount emphasized the script and budget. Lee viewed it as a 10 million dollar picture, while Paramount intended to invest only 8 million with a proviso that the ending be changed. As negotiations continued, the Paramount production executives Ned Tannen, Sid Gannis, and Gary Luchesi repeatedly urged Lee to change the potentially volatile ending. "They are convinced that Black people will come out of the theaters wanting to burn shit down" (*DRT*, p. 76). According to Lee:

Ned Tannen, the president, has big problems with the end of the picture, especially Sal's line about Blacks being smarter

because they don't burn down their own houses anymore. . . .
They want an ending that they feel won't incite a giant Black
uprising. (*DRT,* p. 76)

In addition to the battle over the script, there were questions
concerning the amount of money the studio would make if the
film were to explore controversial, only marginally profitable
issues. Few films are produced by Hollywood majors in which a
lead white male character loses to his African-American male
rival. Sure, Rocky lost to Apollo Creed and Clubber Lang, but
who won the climactic fight in every Rocky film? Similarly, in
the Blaxploitation period, pioneered by the films *Sweet
Sweetback's Baadasssss Song* (1971) and *Superfly* (1972), success
came at a price. The majority of subsequent films were not about
"beating the man," "mista charley," or whatever you want to
call him, nor were they about improving the lives of black folks.
Usually they were about African-Americans falling deeper into
despair and doing little or nothing to change their predicament.

Regardless of how one feels about his films, Spike Lee has
helped to make significant changes in the way the film industry
deals with African-Americans. Before Lee and the Paramount
executives arrived at their final impasse in negotiations, Bill
Horborg, another Paramount executive, tried to find a resolution
satifactory to both Spike Lee and Ned Tannen. With negotiations
deteriorating, Lee sent a script to Katzenberg at Touchstone Pictures, the studio that originally wanted *School Daze.* Thirteen
days before Paramount rejected the *DRT* project, Jeffrey Katzenberg informed Lee that Touchstone was not interested in the
project. Katzenberg believed the film was not worth the budget
Lee wanted. After the two rejections, Lee responded, "I kinda
figured that they were taking too long. Bill Horborg fought for
me till the end. But he's not Ned Tannen. . . . Goes to show you,
take nothing for granted till the check is in the bank and has
cleared" (*DRT,* p. 80).

Paramount and Touchstone had already turned down *DRT*
and it was crucial for Lee to follow up *School Daze* with another

film. While any filmmaker feels the need to obtain a production budget that exceeds the budget for his or her last film, it is especially important for African-American filmmakers to succeed at this. According to Lee, "This is crucial; no recent Black filmmaker has been able to go from film to film as the white boys do" (*DRT*, p. 79).

By this time Spike Lee and his lawyer, Arthur Klein, had already made contact with Sam Kitt in the acquisitions department at Universal Studios. Universal agreed to finance *DRT* but told Lee that the budget would be lower than the 8 million dollar minimum he had sought in earlier *DRT* negotiations. Lee's negotiations with Universal were more concerned with how to stretch the money than with increasing the budget, but there was an upside to dealing with Universal. The studio was willing to stand behind the script. The studio had already generated controversy when it released Martin Scorsese's *Last Temptation of Christ* (1988). Nonetheless, Universal was attracted to Lee because he had a small but successful body of films that were not only profitable but had come in under budget. Tom Pollock, head of Universal Pictures, had this to say:

> We're not some crusading studio out looking for social issues. Spike is interested in the subject matter and so are we. . . . But we can't afford to make movies if we can't make money on them.[6]

On the basis of Spike Lee's first efforts at the box office, Universal felt it was making a pretty safe bet. *School Daze* was a box-office success despite Columbia Pictures' lack of promotional support. Lee is a filmmaker whose name alone has the potential to sell tickets. He thus represents a traditional, tried-and-true market commodity: the big-name director, in his own way a throwback to the likes of John Ford, Howard Hawks, and Alfred Hitchcock.

It is an unfortunate fact that Blacks who work in the U.S. film industry have very few friends in high places. Perhaps this is also true for other people of color. Nevertheless, any film studio that finances a project rejected by other major competitors in the industry not only takes a major risk, but also performs an admirable task. Not only was Universal willing to take a chance but, as Lee would later discover, Tom Pollock, the chief at Universal, would give him unrelenting support.

Lee's decision to go with Universal in the wake of failed negotiations elsewhere was probably an easy one to make. Universal offered the money to make the film and allowed Lee to retain artistic control, as well as some degree of financial control. The negotiations that transpired at Universal could not have been more different from those at Paramount. Lee and Klein got Universal to agree with most of their demands. Lee had the final cut and a mutual agreement over the casting. These issues may seem minor, but they can make or break a film. For example, in the making of *The Godfather* (1972), Paramount Pictures did not want Francis Ford Coppola to cast Marlon Brando and Al Pacino in the roles of Vito Corleone and his son Michael. How wrong the studio bosses were. Even today, despite all of the great roles that Brando has played, people remember him as much for *The Godfather* as for any other film. Spike Lee did what he should as the director and took the responsible position. If *DRT* was going to succeed or fail, it would be his doing.

PREPRODUCTION, FILM TRADE UNIONS, AND *DRT*

Although financing for the film was secured, its production would face a series of hurdles. Here was a man with a short but admirable track record. Lee's thesis film, *Joe's Bed-Stuy Barbershop: We Cut Heads* (1982), won the student Academy Award and his first feature, *She's Gotta Have It,* not only won the Prix de Jeunesse at the Cannes Film Festival, but based on box-office receipts of $8 million made more than forty times its production costs of $175,000. Lee's talent and determination were already indisputable. Critic Nelson George, who helped to finance *She's Gotta Have It,* pointed out, "I invested because it was shot already. Spike wasn't talking *doing,* he was talking *done.*"[7]

Universal agreed to finance Lee's film for $7.5 million and to shoot in New York City, which is strongly controlled by the film trade unions. *DRT* would be Lee's first union film, and he would experience difficulties with the unions. Lee wanted a nonunion shoot for the entire ten weeks of shooting. His cinematographer, Ernest Dickerson, expressed concern that a nonunion shoot in New York would cause problems. John Kilik, the line producer, was responsible for coming up with a budget that would work. In addition, Lee needed approval on a budget, so he made the decision to have John Kilik draw up a nonunion budget of less than $7.5 million, that figure being the maximum to which he believed Universal would commit itself. The revised budget came in at $5.5 million, and Arthur Klein forwarded it to Universal. Universal suggested a change of venue, which was its way of saying no more money.

Even though Universal had agreed in principle to finance the film, a final budget had not been reached. When Lee firmly decided that *DRT* would be shot in Brooklyn or not at all, he forced Universal either to accept his decision or to reject the whole project. Thereby, Lee entered into a second significant waiting period in which he actually thought Universal would drop *DRT.* The studio proposed a budget of $6 million even though Lee insisted that it was a $7.5 million picture. At this point, he was prepared to start shopping again and consulted Klein about giving Orion Pictures a copy of his script. When Universal finally settled on a budget, Spike was not pleased. The terms included a $6.5 million budget, a union crew, and a shooting schedule cut from ten weeks to eight. Lee wrote:

> Universal is dicking me around. They won't budge from the $6.5 million budget, won't go a penny over it. It's ridiculous. White boys get real money, fuck up, lose millions of dollars, and still get chance after chance. Not so with us. You fuck up one time, that's it. After the commercial successes of *She's*

Gotta Have It and *School Daze,* I shouldn't have to fight for the pennies the way I'm doing now. But what else can I do? I'll make the best film possible with the budget I'm given. (*DRT*, p. 87)

Because Universal wouldn't budge from $6.5 million, Lee had no choice but to negotiate with the unions. A union shoot in New York would be problematic for several reasons. First, a sizable portion of the $6.5 million budget would have to be earmarked for an all-union crew. Second, Lee wanted to hire more than one or two Blacks, a nearly impossible task since African-American members are seriously underrepresented in the film trade unions. Lee wrote:

On every film, I try to use as many black people as possible. A major concern I had about shooting with an all-union crew was whether this would prevent me from hiring as many blacks as I wanted. There are few minorities in the film unions, and, historically, film unions have done little to encourage Blacks and women to join their ranks. (*DRT*, p. 99)

Although Lee was not able to have a nonunion crew, he succeeded in getting the National Association of Broadcast Employees and Technicians and the International Brotherhood of Teamsters to hire a few African-American nonunion workers for the shoot. Both unions made major concessions that included offering membership to the African-American nonunion workers who filled positions primarily in the grip and electric departments. These gestures by the unions may seem generous, but actually solid business decisions lurked behind them. A local union should do all it can to keep work among its own. Thus, the union's opening of its membership to African-Americans benefited all parties involved.

Despite Universal Pictures' insistence that Lee shoot the film somewhere other than Brooklyn, Lee would not budge. "Universal suggested we shoot the film someplace outside New York, like Philadelphia or Baltimore. I'm sorry, Philly and Baltimore are great cities, but they just aren't Brooklyn" (*DRT*, p. 107). Eight years ago, after reading the companion volume to *DRT*, I thought Lee was foolishly stubborn. Now I realize that although most major cities have significant African-American populations, the African-American urban folk cultures differ from city to city. This point is demonstrated by regional differences in rap music. The West Coast has produced a minimal lyrical style with a focus on the music, a style built on 1970s funk music. In contrast, East Coast rappers focus mainly on the lyrical aspects and produce new music by rearranging pieces and bits of songs from a smorgasbord of sounds. South Central Los Angeles does not produce the same musical culture as found in New York's Brooklyn, the Bronx, and uptown Manhattan.

Lee was determined to shoot the film in the heart of Bed-Stuy. He sent out a location scout to find one block to use for filming. After two weeks had passed, Lee and the film's production designer, Thomas, chose the first block the scout had recommended. Lee thought the location was perfect. It was neither too dilapidated nor too upscale. It also had two empty lots on opposite corners that were perfect locations for Wynn Thomas to create the focal buildings in the film – Sal's Famous Pizzeria, the Korean grocery, and the We Love Radio 108 FM storefront station. After choosing a neighborhood, Lee wanted to communicate freely with its inhabitants. Securing a block for a shoot is not usually that difficult. You obtain the proper permits and, maybe, grease a palm or two. This location shoot, however, would present more complications than usual. Most films have multiple locations over the duration of shooting. *DRT*, however, would be shot at one location for eight weeks. Concerned that the presence of police and the use of permits during preparation of the location would perhaps anger the African-American residents, Lee took a more diplomatic approach, which Brent Owens, the location manager, describes:

During pre-production we scheduled a meeting for homeowners on the block. We went over our production schedule and discussed the improvements planned on several homes. Everyone seemed pleased that we were there. Shutting down the crack houses won us some points with the homeowners. They were much more willing to lease us their property after we did that.[8]

Instead of using a traditional security force, Lee, upon producer Monty Ross's suggestion, hired the Fruit of Islam (FOI), the security force of the Nation of Islam, originally trained by Malcolm X. Because the FOI has bettered the lives of many African-Americans from all walks of life, they have acquired the respect of those who live in black inner-city communities. With the FOI, Lee would have a security force better suited to *DRT*'s needs than the New York City Police Department could provide. The FOI entered peacefully into the Bed-Stuy, assessed the security problems, and rid the shooting location of any unwanted elements. Some reporters who covered this angle criticized what they perceived to be the failings of the FOI. Apparently, the FOI closed down three crack houses but one moved around the corner and went back into business. Some journalists viewed this reopening as an example of the FOI's ineffectiveness.

Spike Lee made great advances with *DRT* that should not be taken lightly. Lee served notice to Hollywood that the rules must change. He knew that at some point a major studio would give him a larger budget to work with. With each new project, Lee has been able to increase his production budget. His budgets, however, remain low in comparison with average production budgets for other Hollywood fare. For instance, in 1989 the average budget for studio-produced films was $18 million. Lee is struggling for economic empowerment for African-Americans and the opportunity for other African-Americans to make films. To date, four of the crew members from *DRT*, Darnell Martin, Monty Ross, Ernest Dickerson, and Preston Holmes, have produced, written, and/or directed their own feature films. Moreover, Lee was instrumental in integrating the trade unions, getting them to use African-American nonunion technicians and filmmakers who would later become active union members and skilled artists.

WAKE UP, WAKE UP, UP YA WAKE

"Sal, that might be fine, you own this, but rarely do I see any Italian-Americans eating in here. All I've ever seen is black folks. So since we spend much money here, we do have some say."

(Buggin' Out in *DRT*)

DRT was a serendipitous combination of excellent filmmaking and a timely issue that has grown in significance since the film's release. The Clarence Thomas–Anita Hill hearings, the Rodney King affair, and, most recently, the O. J. Simpson trial have reasserted the questions dramatized in *DRT*.

DRT's achievement lies in Spike Lee's ability to surmount obstacles and deal evenly with the issue of racism, both in front of and behind the camera. From the outset, he rejected the film industry's suggestions that he make a film about black-on-black crime in a drug-infested neighborhood. If he had accepted such a project, the studio would surely have granted him a much larger production budget. Now many post-*DRT* films dramatize drug dealers and violence, yet Lee refused to present these issues in *DRT*.[9] The recent cycle of black gangster films have romanticized the drug dealers and gang violence that plague black urban America. These films focus on one situation and provide a very narrow view of the black urban experience.

DRT reminds us that doing the right thing always involves recognizing interracial discord and attempting to eradicate the socioeconomic problems that produce it. For African-Americans, there exist additional right things to do, such as working within the black community to find solutions. *DRT* dramatizes a difficult and perplexing issue that the United States must resolve: how to reapportion psychological, social, and economic space

FIGURE 4

Sal (Danny Aiello), the owner of Sal's Famous Pizzeria in *Do the Right Thing*. (Courtesy of the Museum of Modern Art, New York.)

for both the individual and various racial and ethnic communities. The resolution of this contemporary political problem will surely promote the betterment of society. Hopefully, Lee will continue to explore these questions throughout his career.

NOTES

1. David Denby, "He's Gotta Have It," *New York* (June 26, 1989): 53–54.
2. In *Five For Five: The Films of Spike Lee* (New York: Stewart, Tabori and Chang, 1991), Lee writes, "*Daze* was a real movie; *She's Gotta* had been made mostly with friends and relatives and $175,000. *Daze* was 6.5 million bucks" (p. 14).
3. Pamela Johnson, "They've Gotta Have It," *Black Enterprise* (July 1989): 36–44.

4. Spike Lee with Lisa Jones, *Do the Right Thing: A Spike Lee Joint* (New York: Simon & Schuster, 1989), p. 31. In this essay, all subsequent references to this book are noted in the text by *DRT* and page number.

5. Johnson, "They've Gotta Have It," pp. 36–44.

6. Quoted in Jack Mathews, "The Cannes File: Controversial Film for a Long Hot Summer," *Los Angeles Times* (May 22, 1989), home ed., p. 1.

7. Johnson, "They've Gotta Have It," p. 38.

8. Lee with Jones, *Do the Right Thing,* photo section.

9. Lee treats black-on-black violence and drug dealing in *Jungle Fever* (1991) and *Clockers* (1995).

CATHERINE POUZOULET

2 The Cinema of Spike Lee
IMAGES OF A MOSAIC CITY

political science
↳ social science → sociology

Before the release of *Malcolm X* had redirected critical attention at Spike Lee, the May 1992 Los Angeles uprising sharpened the relevance of Lee's political message. Within the corpus of Lee's five films, *Do the Right Thing* seemed the most inclined to reveal the political underpinnings of Lee's cinema, which had been so far inherently subversive. In retrospect, Los Angeles *theatrical* somehow vindicated Spike Lee, whose deliberate, aesthetically *artist* pleasing vision had been derided as a theatricalization rather *↳ high* than a "real" depiction of black sociopolitics. Critics pitted Lee's *saturation* black aesthetic against the sociological concerns of another black movie maker, John Singleton, who in *Boyz N the Hood* shows the dissolution of the ghetto, yet fails to dramatize the important issue that is central to *DTR* – the struggles for power within the city. However, any serious analysis of *DTR* requires a discussion of the film's relationship to the filmmaker, Lee.

It is widely acknowledged that Lee courts and then provokes the white establishment with an irritating insolence that reflects on the reception of his cinema. Lee has become a sought-after spokesman for the African-American community, and his film journals discuss his cinematic politics of black identity. He, however, is quick to deny a "racialized" legitimacy. The general pop-

31

FIGURE 5
The four faces of Mookie (Spike Lee). *Upper left:* Agent for Nike athletic gear. *Upper right:* The bedroom-eyes lover of Tina (Rosie Perez). *Lower left:* Pizza delivery man. *Lower right:* Filmmaker of *Do the Right Thing.* (From the editor's collection.)

ularity and commercial success of Lee's films among both black and nonblack audiences make him a mediator between the African-American community and the white establishment. It permits him to have his love–hate relationship with the American film industry. One can possibly transcend Lee's ambiguity by tracing how his films construct a racialized territory. This

essay analyzes Lee's cinematic aesthetic by discussing the forma-
tion of territorial roots.

THE TERRITORIAL INSCRIPTION OF SPIKE
LEE'S FILMS

With the exception of the southern setting of *School
Daze* and some Harlem scenes in *Mo' Better Blues* and *Jungle Fever,*
Brooklyn has been Spike Lee's favorite shooting location. Lee
himself never fails to emphasize his Brooklyn roots. Brooklyn is
where he grew up and still lives, although he resides with other
upwardly mobile young artists and professionals in gentrified
neighborhoods in the Fort Greene section near Brooklyn
Heights. This is also the neighborhood where his film production company, Forty Acres and a Mule, and his retail store, Spike
Lee Joint, are located.

Lee's use of Brooklyn is not accidental. The most densely
populated of New York City's five boroughs (2.2 million inhabitants out of a total New York City population of more than 7
million), Brooklyn is the home of more than half of New York
City's African-American population. Today, Brooklyn, not Harlem, qualifies as a black metropolis.[1] Brooklyn best illustrates
what Marcel Roncayolo, a French geographer, calls the palimp-
sest dimension of the city in its superimposition of past remains
and traces of the present.[2] Its gentrified sections are populated
predominantly by affluent whites. There are interracial neighborhoods where new immigrants have joined the ranks of
African-Americans and Hispanics; there are also Jewish and Italian enclaves and older white working-class neighborhoods that
are undergoing racial and economic transitions. Yet, from this
astounding patchwork, which has earned New York the designa-
tion "the mosaic city," Spike Lee retains a highly selective vision
of Brooklyn, an image stilled in time and space. In *DRT,* he films
a story about one day in the life of a block in the Bedford-
Stuyvesant section of Brooklyn. And starting from a tangible
reality (the film was actually shot on Stuyvesant Avenue between

Quincy Street and Lexington Avenue), Spike Lee performs a se-ries of manipulations that artfully transform a very real setting into a theatrical stage. On this stage, his didactic vision projects itself onto the silver screen. By choosing to situate his film in "Bed-Stuy," Lee brings a new slant to filmed and televised images of Brooklyn. He chooses an area of Brooklyn that symbolizes the black ghetto with its substandard housing and record-high number of welfare recipients. Yet Lee's black ghetto is not devas-tated by poverty, unemployment, and drug abuse.[3] If Lee's styl-ized Bed-Stuy is so different from the Los Angeles ghetto de-picted by filmmaker John Singleton, it is because Lee's aesthetic concerns deliberately overshadow the depth and intensity of racial and economic exclusion.

Public Enemy, Lee's "favorite politically conscious rappers,"[4] provides lyrics to underline the film's politics of resistance – "Fight the Powers That Be." Visually, DRT is painted in "Afrocen-tric bright" colors.[5] At Lee's shoot, an inner-city neighborhood, there was an absence of drug use and street gangs thanks to the work of the Fruit of Islam, which kept local hoodlums and drug dealers at a safe distance from the shooting location.[6]

The images of Blacks and Latinos are demographically skewed in DRT since native-born African-Americans and Puerto Ricans are decreasing in relative number compared with New York's general black and Latino population. Currently, Puerto Ricans make up less than half the New York Latino population, and the overall black population includes 25 percent foreign-born Blacks. In spite of these demographic shifts, Lee depicts a mono-lithic black community. DRT includes young Puerto Ricans, but Bed-Stuy, in the heart of the "dark" ghetto,[7] is even more atypi-cal of Brooklyn in that Whites make up only about 2 percent of its population. Thus, the African-American population domi-nates (87.3 percent), and though Puerto Ricans are visible, they remain a definite minority (8.3 percent), while Asians (at 0.8 percent) and other recent immigrants (1.5 percent) have an even smaller presence.[8]

The interethnic chessboard of *DRT,* therefore, offers a warped *main character is the neighborhood.* vision of the actual social scene in the 1990s. Other than the single character of the Korean grocer, the new immigrants are little more than extras. Managing his own business and making a good living, the grocer acts as a foil to his African-American patrons stuck at the bottom rungs of the social ladder. Spike Lee is deliberately provocative when he has three black men voice resentment against the Korean: Lee thereby suggests that these men clearly lack enterprise. He almost echoes the criticism that neoconservatives have directed against Blacks who are dependent on federal entitlements and welfare programs. Yet it is significant that Lee does not recirculate stereotypes such as the unemployed, murderous, drug-dealing black youth. Rather, he portrays the three black men as likable, happy-go-lucky characters who are simply shorter on deeds than words. His three "corner men" act as a chorus that offers ongoing commentary on the neighborhood.

In contrast to these working-class characters is one middle-class Euro-American. Clifton, the yuppie owner of a brownstone, is a quite improbable figure in Bed-Stuy. He is presented as a third-generation white ethnic born in Brooklyn and raised in the suburbs who has decided to return to the city. The scene in which he carries his bike up his stoop and accidentally steps on Buggin' Out's new sneakers and soils them is an inside joke for those familiar with the Michael Jordan television commercial. In this black community, being "dressed to kill" means wearing popular sneakers and other accessories and being ready to kill anyone who disrespects them.[9] The verbal altercation between Clifton and Buggin' Out's friends does not degenerate into violence, somewhat unconvincingly, but this encounter is one of several interracial altercations with nonblacks that increase racial tensions up to the murder of Radio Raheem and the destruction of Sal's pizzeria.

Sal's pizzeria is a distinct remnant of the past. Sal and his sons do not live in the neighborhood where the pizzeria is located but in Bensonhurst. In fact, in the actual Bedford-Stuyvesant section of Brooklyn in which the film is shot, an Italian-run business would be a curiosity.

Last, the block lives under the scrutiny of a patrol of white policemen who don't even try to conceal their deep contempt when they coolly observe the three street-corner men sitting idly under their beach umbrella, talking their heads off day in, day out. The tension generated by the oversight of the neighborhood by these insensitive, potentially racist white cops is exaggerated to the point of caricature. Police forces, though still a white bastion, have been significantly integrated in the past twenty years, so that, especially in the ghetto, a patrol today is very unlikely to consist of Whites only.

Surreptitiously filtered through Spike Lee's didactic lenses, the confrontation between African-Americans and a white society ethnicized into Italians, Jews, and Irish is magnified, although it reflects the context of the late 1960s much more accurately than the present situation, in which Blacks are increasingly confronted in their neighborhoods by other American ethnic minorities as well as newly arrived immigrants. But far from being a vision inadvertently inherited from a vanished past, this obsessive, permanent confrontation between Blacks and Whites best reflects one aspect of New York City life: the political arena, where the black community struggles to assert itself against a white political establishment, still in a position to dominate the decision-making process in spite of the fact that New York City has become a majority of minorities.

THE POLITICAL BACKGROUND OF *DO THE RIGHT THING*: THE (RE)CONQUEST OF POWER

Spike Lee's film is replete with references to a series of racial incidents that polarized New York and sharpened interethnic tensions. The film is dedicated to the families of victims of police brutality: Eleanor Bumpurs, an old black woman who was evicted from her apartment; Michael Stewart, strangled like Ra-

FIGURE 6

Spike Lee, the director and writer of *Do the Right Thing*, wants a new mayor for New York City. (From the editor's collection.)

dio Raheem by a choke hold; Arthur Miller, a black entrepreneur who was the victim of mistaken identities, unjustly arrested and beaten up, and, in 1978, died as a result of the beating. Arthur Miller's death prompted Reverend Herbert Daughtry, a neighborhood preacher, to found the Black United Front, which is still active in New York City politics. The film also makes explicit references to incidents of interethnic violence, such as the killing of Michael Griffith, who, as he was leaving a pizzeria in the predominantly white Howard Beach section of Queens, was fatally beaten by Italian-American youths armed with baseball bats. Michael Griffith's death mobilized the African-American community. Reverend Daughtry and other community activists staged a day of protest, called a "Day of Rage," which was organized around a march across the Brooklyn Bridge. By his own account, this incident triggered Spike Lee's idea for *DRT* and provided him with a basic iconography, although he transposed the scene from Queens to Brooklyn. And in the climatic scene when Sal's pizzeria is looted, the black youths wreck the place as they shout "Howard Beach." The film, therefore, provides two perspectives: the references to racial incidents and their direct link to former New York mayor Ed Koch's divisive ethnic politics. The film should be read against the background of the 1989 New York mayoral campaign, which resulted in the election of David Dinkins and the rejection of Mayor Ed Koch, a three-term incumbent, who had become extremely unpopular within the black community. To understand the historical importance of Lee's film, one must first understand the neoconservative politics of the Koch administration, which laid the foundation for the reign of interethnic hatred and murders that Lee suggestively portrays in *DRT*.

In 1977, the election of Ed Koch signaled the renewal of the electorate's concern for the white middle class. The Koch 1977 campaign created a pro-growth coalition with New York business elites so Koch could implement a policy of fiscal retrenchment that would eliminate many of New York's liberal social programs.[10] Koch attacked his predecessor, John Lindsay, for his excessive clientelist policies and held them responsible for the fiscal crisis that left New York on the verge of bankruptcy in 1975. New York City's predicament revealed to a stunned nation the economic crisis that would later be shared by other major U.S. cities.[11] Former mayor John Lindsay had indeed confronted social unrest as well as the pent-up demands of the large municipal work force that New York, like all other major municipal governments, had to develop to meet the needs of a large, increasingly heterogeneous population.[12] As the suburbs prospered at the expense of major urban centers, the social and economic disparities between cities and their suburbs widened, and the cities, by the 1970s, became fiscally vulnerable. The forces that prompted middle-class workers to move outside city limits also kept a large number of the poor in the inner cities. A disproportionate number of minority households became socially isolated and increasingly dependent on public welfare programs.[13] Consequently, there was an increased demand for municipal services, which fueled the urban fiscal crisis after the city tax base had eroded.[14]

By the 1970s, New York was not only fiscally vulnerable; its inhabitants had become even more subject to the whims of politicians and business leaders seeking fiscally responsible programs. To reestablish and stabilize New York City's fiscal health, Mayor Koch adopted a rhetoric of boosterism and pushed for downtown redevelopment strategies that focused on tourism (for example, the "I Love New York" campaign), conventions, downtown retailing, and the construction of midtown office buildings and luxury apartments. The assumption was that these redevelopment incentives, fueled by all kinds of tax exemptions, would attract private investors to Manhattan and create a good business climate for pulling the city out of its economic doldrums. Mayor Koch's plan did, in fact, bring about an economic turnaround; unfortunately, it affected only the corporate business world, failing to foster community-wide prosperity.[15] The upper middle and upper classes prospered from Manhattan's economic restructuring, but impoverished Blacks and Hispanics as well as the displaced manufacturing workers were increasingly locked out of the economic mainstream. It was this ethnically mixed group of New Yorkers who faced shrinking economic opportunities and increasing neighborhood distress.

Mayor Koch's "blame the victim" attitude was demoralizing in the context of growing social inequalities between highly skilled professionals and the increasingly unskilled workers who were cut out when New York received its economic face lift. Despite these blatant inequities, Koch's demagogy made him quite popular among white conservative working-class Catholics and Jews in the outer boroughs.[16] African-Americans, whose political coming-of-age under former mayor John Lindsay's administration had not yet translated into an institutionalized, long-term presence, found themselves marginalized.

Repeated failures in 1981 and 1985 to win back the mayoralty were evidence of the black community's political weakness. Plagued by inner strife, it was unable to reach out to Latinos and build a progressive coalition. After these electoral defeats, the time was ripe in 1989 to "do the right thing," a formidable rallying cry that reverberated throughout the summer and was adopted by the New York hospital workers' Local 1199 as their motto. In September, the union organized a huge protest meeting at Riverside Church, which attracted many local and national black politicians such as David Dinkins and Jesse Jackson. By the time *DRT* was released in 1989, the New York City mayoral campaign had already turned ugly, as reflected in the film's final intertitle, "The election is near!" This exclamatory statement is Spike Lee's implicit encouragement to his audience to vote for David Dinkins.

Today, the black Brooklyn community is at the forefront of a new type of activism that has resulted from alliances between progressive politicians working with religious leaders, local activists, and trade unionists. These people have formed a political community outside the traditional scope of elected black politicians who are beholden to the Democratic Party. Reverend Herbert Daughtry, a symbolic and real-life figure who marries Bleek and Indigo at the end of Lee's *Mo' Better Blues,* is the very embodiment of black Brooklyn's political activism as it attempts to reconcile the two schools of black political nationalism – cultural and radical. This activism has emerged from the debates of the late 1960s to transcend its philosophical divisions and seek a common strategy for black political empowerment and black community control over its socioeconomic life.

Such a strategy will nonetheless always be self-defeating unless previously untapped electoral resources, a pool of potential new voters, is politically mobilized within the black community, and this cannot be achieved without a socialization process as well. *DRT* shows the economic exclusion of African-Americans but shuns any portrayal of the social pathologies that such economic deprivations engender. Paradoxically, the film has be-

come a trademark of life in the ghetto. I contend that in *DRT*
there is a refusal to depict realistically deviant behavioral patterns, and this is Lee's penultimate political mistake. His message
should express the need to transcend all forms of gratuitous, self-
destructive violence. The looting of Sal's pizzeria brings about
the disappearance of the only space in which neighborhood
youths meet in a convivial way – a place where they might
create multiethnic alliances for higher socioeconomic stakes and
thereby become serious social activists.

This process raises the larger issue of the symbolic (de)con-
struction of space. Under the pretense of an aesthetic vision,
Spike Lee gives us a re-presentation of a black ghetto that is also
a black neighborhood (I am here referring to the traditional
sense of "neighborhood" – a place complete with a sense of time
and space), one that has not yet deteriorated into what the
French anthropologist Marc Auge calls a *non-lieu*, that is, a non-
existent place, a sort of wasteland.[17] As the "utter negation of
utopia," Auge claims that a "*non-lieu* . . . exists but fails to shelter
any organic society."[18] Spike Lee is fully aware that depicting the
ghetto as a regular neighborhood, with its families, social life,
and characters, as it no longer exists, is in fact more disturbing
to mainstream audiences than adopting the sort of realistic approach John Singleton used in *Boyz N the Hood*.

In a country where the antiurban bias is so strong that most
people, including politicians, seem resigned to having a nation
of cities in crisis, cities are no longer viewed as important for the
health of the nation.[19] Indifference to the plight of the inner
cities is even greater. The fact, clearly demonstrated by all the
scholarly literature, that the socially polarized and divided cities
of the global society have been shaped primarily by market
forces and reinforced by federal policies remains largely ignored
by the general public. Throughout the Reagan–Bush years,
middle-class Americans were encouraged to secede from the los-
ers. Spike Lee reminds them that the social costs of economic
restructuring are very real and disproportionately borne by racial
minorities. Something must be done about it. Economist Richard

Knight believes that a "civic awareness" has to emerge.[20] Surely, it is an uphill battle for those who fight against indifference to the plight of the urban centers. Knight says that "cities do not have an urban vision nor think of themselves as having the power to shape their own destinies."[21] Yet he quickly counters such pessimism: "Divided cities are not inevitable, they are created by default. Cities have a choice: they can allow market forces and technology to dictate development and become divided cities or they can shape development through the civic process and secure a future in the global society."[22]

Obviously, this comprehensive approach to cities is only dawning because, as Peter Salins explains, it implies a debunking of "the Faustian metropolitan bargain" that made segregation economically and socially functional for metropolitan businesses and residents. He writes, "The cities agreed to serve increasingly as the poorhouses of the metropolitan community, as long as the suburbanites – with Washington and the state capitals acting as brokers and intermediaries – underwrite the extra costs this role imposes."[23] The belief that "cities are an optional feature of the US economic landscape," and that in the new posturban America most people can find not only their homes but their livelihoods in the suburbs, is even a more formidable obstacle than years of unfair and shortsighted policies. The prejudice against cities is so deeply rooted in mainstream public opinion that "their economic obsolescence is for many Americans something to cheer rather than to lament."[24] The cosmopolitan nature of the modern metropolis was, from the first, alien to the two dominant representations of the American ideal, identified by Thomas Bender as the communitarian myth of the U.S. town and the agrarian myth of the U.S. landscape.[25] Both myths emphasized sameness and homogeneity and reflected weariness with the immorality and deviance associated with urban life. Jefferson had articulated most forcefully this deep distrust of cities, which he claimed to be "sores upon the body politic." The escape to suburbia, a "refuge between the decadent city and the howling wilderness,"[26] can thus be traced to the beginning of the nineteenth century, when the largest cities underwent a dramatic spatial change and promoted "a new pattern of suburban affluence and center of despair."[27] Initially, the impetus to retreat to the suburbs was prompted by the desire to *Idealized* find a refuge from the untidy, chaotic, immigrant-ridden cities in a pastoral, bucolic environment. In the postwar period, when suburban migration became an option open not only to the affluent but to the middle classes, and a mass phenomenon, an ideology of suburban desirability and city avoidance revived the antiurban attitude that had taken shape during the formative years of the nation. And the pastoral ideal came to be reinterpreted as the suburban lifestyle, while cities were in contrast viewed as sites of decay and degeneracy.[28] This dominant discourse, which cites the decline of cities versus the growth and prosperity of the suburbs, has deep political implications. It allows suburbanites to feel not only indifference, but relief at having escaped the city and its self-destructive ghettos.[29] But if there is one lesson to be learned from the May 1992 civil disturbances in Los Angeles, it was aptly stated by Henry Cisneros following his visit to the riot-torn area: "The white-hot intensity that became Los Angeles was the combustion of smoldering embers waiting impatiently to ignite for a long time."[30] Other cities can easily ignite, as Spike Lee imaginatively demonstrated in *DRT*.

Most critics interpreted the movie's conclusion as an irresponsible encouragement to enact violence: the character impersonated by Spike Lee, Mookie, happens to be the one who initiates the riot by hurling a trash can through the window of Sal's pizzeria; this leads to the looting and burning of Sal's business. Though critics have emphasized the fact that by channeling black anger at Sal's property Mookie saved Sal's life, they have also viewed Mookie's diversionary tactics as advocating violence. Spike Lee ends his movie with apparently contradictory quotations from Martin Luther King and Malcolm X, which advocate, respectively, peaceful change and the use of retaliatory violence as a means of self-defense. Yet the choice between nonviolence *final sequence*

Final sequence

and retaliatory violence has no relevance to the working poor who are economically trapped in gang-infested urban ghettos. Spike Lee's political message was premonitory as the American Assembly concluded its final report on the plight of U.S. cities: "We create the conditions of social unrest when we fail to address pent-up anger and frustration."[31]

Is it an ethical act.

"BROOKLYN: DO OR DIE" – RACIAL IDENTITY AND COMMUNITY

Spike Lee has been sharply criticized for his romanticized vision of a clean and apparently drug- and crime-free Bed-Stuy where teenagers and unemployed young males congregate on brownstone stoops. Critics have rightly asked if Lee's *DRT* creates a mythic ghetto, a wishful "kinder, gentler urban America."[32] Admittedly, Lee "made a conscious decision not to discuss drugs,"[33] and this would have been acceptable had he not ignored the larger socioeconomic reality – the urban blight – that greets the visitor entering Bed-Stuy. With the exception of *Jungle Fever* and its dualistic representation of two brothers, the successful buppie Flipper and his crack-cocaine-addicted brother, Gator, Lee's pre-1995 films avoid depicting drug dealing in the black community. Four years after *Jungle Fever*, Lee's *Clockers* would openly confront the drug problem that has devastated black urban communities for the past twenty years. The hard-fought battles against residential segregation and unfair employment practices benefited the black middle class, which eventually escaped the overcrowded and badly maintained housing in the urban ghettos. The black ghetto has experienced two successive population movements: the first, in the earlier part of the century, brought an influx of southern rural Blacks into northern cities in search of better living conditions; the second, in the late 1960s, was an exodus of the black middle class from the inner cities as a result of the integrationist, legalistic strategy pursued by black elites from the turn of the century. This strategy proved ineffective in dismantling the barriers of de facto

Writing of the Ghetto

segregation and economic dependence. Deprived of its middle and upper classes, black inner-city neighborhoods remain caught in a cycle of sociocultural destruction[34] that fosters drug dealing, gang warfare, and the destruction of black families.

Spike Lee's generation is the immediate heir to the political and cultural legacy of the Civil Rights movement, which is evident in his iconographic use of Dr. Martin Luther King, Jr., and Malcolm X in *DRT* and many of his other films. Lee preaches racial pride, but Buggin' Out represents someone who wastes his energy on lost causes. By contrast, Da Mayor, a friendly old drunkard, is a valued spokesman of worldly wisdom and a repository of bedrock values. The difference in Lee's treatment of Buggin' Out and Da Mayor suggests that, in the absence of black entrepreneurs and a political agency, one can still maintain Da Mayor's sense of decency. By showing people who are poor but who have nonetheless retained their dignity, Lee goes against the easy clichés that sustain conservative attacks on the welfare state. If, however, *DRT* had presented a realistic vision of Bed-Stuy, it would have reinforced the paranoia of many middle-class Americans who fear the day when poverty and homelessness will invade their well-insulated neighborhoods that are far from inner cities and its crime. *DRT* bolsters the more or less imaginary class and racial boundaries between certain Blacks and Whites who view the cities in fantastic terms, with marauding youth gangs in control of their increasingly monitored "public" spaces.[35] Mike Davis claims that as long as the actual violence is more or less confined to the ghetto, gang wars, as shown in *Boyz N the Hood*, are a "voyeuristic titillation to white suburbanites."[36] By showing an alternative to *Boyz N the Hood*'s throwaway ghetto, where a whole generation is doomed to a social if not physical death, and the middle-class suburbia of a privatized "citadel" city, Spike Lee's *DRT* raises the issue of the territoriality crisis of in an African-American urban community. He implies that those who accept the failure of the Great Society and the ineffectiveness of welfare programs are not "doing the right thing." Lee can therefore claim the legacy of Dr. Martin Luther

King, Jr., and Malcolm X, because their rhetoric and strategies do not contradict but complement each other. The true challenge is to confront what Mike Davis calls the "urban apartheid" and to formulate a policy that does not view self-defense and nonviolence, and separation and integration, as polar opposites. Spike Lee calls for a revitalization of black urban communities through a reappropriation of urban space. A failure to achieve this will perpetuate the present degraded forms of territorial inscription, such as turf wars among street warriors and marauding ethnic vigilantes. These phenomena exacerbate the already oppressive spatial confinement that stifles any quest for economic and spiritual self-betterment and its articulation between the individual and the collective that is a prerequisite of social action.[37]

MEDIATING THE EXPECTATIONS OF BLACKS AND WHITES

Spike Lee's films become less ambiguous when one considers his political message. Despite the apparent contradictions and inconsistencies, a hard look at *DRT* reveals a unifying didactic discourse. Lee constantly interweaves a twofold narrative, manipulating his viewer and striking a responsive chord, alternatively, in Blacks and Whites. This movie was extremely controversial because many people stopped to take a seat in theaters to watch *DRT*. They saw, in the seemingly contradictory characters of Mookie, Buggin' Out, and Radio Raheem, a continuation of the provocative, unsettling behavior Spike Lee generates in real life. If one considers, however, the ideological assumptions that sustain his narrative, then Lee is a mediator rather than an *enfant terrible* of American cinema. In his own way, he follows in the footsteps of Adam Clayton Powell, Jr., another darling of the media and flamboyant spokesman of Harlem, yet another member of the New York African-American community. Powell was once regarded as the living symbol of the black metropolis and was deemed to be in the vanguard of black political activism.[38] Powell and Lee embody the same unusual, volatile qualities and failings that make them either loved or hated as living challenges to the white power elites. The point here is not whether Spike Lee is of comparable stature to the majestic Powell, for whatever one's opinion might be, it merely reflects the contemporary setting in which movie stars, TV anchors, rappers, and black filmmakers are asked their assessment of the "Black Thing." Few black politicians are considered to be qualified leaders in the present crisis. In the aftermath of the May 1992 Los Angeles uprising, black entertainment personalities visited the Los Angeles South Central area and pleaded for a return to calm. Many elected officials prudently stayed away. One may argue that Spike Lee's willingness to be the spokesman for the black community is inherently linked to this ontological dimension of the U.S. dilemma. There might be, however, some danger in crystallizing the frustrations and hopes of a whole community. For as Lee becomes a living metaphor of the socially acceptable African-American courted by the white establishment, he runs the risk of being marginalized or trivialized. This seems to have been the case when his *Malcolm X* created a media stir that was anticlimactic after the movie failed. Yet Spike Lee remains a forceful, multifaceted talent who, by playing upon a facade of social transparence and a racially implicit subtext, attempts to re-create a dialogue between Blacks and Whites.

NOTES

1. In reference to the classic study of the Chicago ghetto see St. Clair Drake and Horace Clayton, *Black Metropolis* (New York: Harper & Row, 1945).
2. In Marcel Roncayolo, *La ville et ses territoires* (Paris: Gallimard, 1990).
3. Michael Stegman, *Housing and Vacancy Report* (New York: City of New York, 1988), p. 164.
4. Quoted by Micah Morrison, "The World According to Spike Lee," *National Review* 41:14 (August 4, 1989): 24.
5. Spike Lee with Lisa Jones, *Do the Right Thing: A Spike Lee Joint* (New York: Simon & Schuster, 1989), p. 29.
6. Ibid., p. 67.

7. Kenneth Clark, *Dark Ghetto: Dilemmas of Social Power* (New York: Harper & Row, 1965). Clark characterizes ghetto life as a tangled pathology.

8. Stegman, *Housing and Vacancy Report,* p. 155.

9. Because of Spike Lee's appearance in Air Jordan commercials, black community leaders have accused him of reinforcing the buying habits of black youths and participating in the rising tide of black-on-black violence among inner-city youths.

10. On the rhetoric of fiscal retrenchment and its ideological appeal see Ester R. Fuchs, *Mayors and Money: Fiscal Policy in New York and Chicago* (Chicago: University of Chicago Press, 1992), pp. 282–90.

11. Paul E. Peterson, "The Changing Fiscal Place of Big Cities in the Federal System," in *Interwoven Destinies: Cities and the Nation,* Henry G. Cisneros ed. (New York: Norton, 1993), pp. 187–210.

12. Richard V. Knight, "City Development and Urbanization: Building the Knowledge-Based City," in *Cities in a Global Society,* Richard V. Knight and Gary Gappart eds., Urban Affairs Annual Reviews, Vol. 35 (Beverly Hills, CA: Sage, 1989), pp. 223–42.

13. Peterson, "The Changing Fiscal Place of Big Cities," p. 191.

14. For similar experiences in Baltimore see Marc Levine, "Urban Redevelopment in a Global Economy: The Cases of Montreal and Baltimore," in *Cities in a Global Society,* pp. 141–52.

15. Saskia Sassen, *The Global City: New York, London, Tokyo* (Princeton, NJ: Princeton University Press, 1991); Rosemary Scanlon, "New York City as Global Capital in the 1980s," in *Cities in a Global Society,* pp. 83–95; and Matthew Drennan, "The Decline and Rise of the New York Economy," in *Dual City: Restructuring New York,* John H. Mollenkopf and Manuel Castells, eds. (New York: Russell Sage Foundation, 1991), pp. 34–46.

16. On the conservative coalition supporting Mayor Ed Koch, see John H. Mollenkopf, *A Phoenix in the Ashes: The Rise and Fall of the Koch Coalition in New York City Politics* (Princeton, NJ: Princeton University Press, 1994).

17. Marc Auge, *Non-lieux: Introduction à une anthropologie de la surmodernité* (Paris: Seuil, 1992), p. 48.

18. Ibid., p. 140.

19. Knight, "City Building in a Global Society," pp. 330–31.

20. Ibid., p. 331.

21. Ibid.

22. See Knight, "City Development and Urbanization," pp. 239–40.

23. Peter Salins, "Metropolitan Areas: Cities, Suburbs and the Ties That Bind," in *Interwoven Destinies,* pp. 162–63.

24. Ibid., pp. 147–48.
25. Jim Sleeper, "New York as a Center of Difference: How America's Metropolis Counters American Myth," *Dissent* 34:4 (Fall 1987): 429–37.
26. James Wunsch, "The Suburban Cliché," *Journal of Social History* 28:3 (Spring 1995): 643.
27. See Kenneth Jackson's discussion of this period in *The Crabgrass Frontier: The Suburbanization of the United States* (New York: Oxford University Press, 1985).
28. Robert Beauregard, "Representing Urban Decline: Postwar Cities as Narrative Objects," *Urban Affairs Quarterly* 29:2 (December 1993): 194.
29. Wunsch, "The Suburban Cliché," p. 656.
30. Henry Cisneros in the opening chapter to *Interwoven Destinies,* p. 19.
31. See the final report to *Interwoven Destinies,* p. 340.
32. Daisann McLane, "Movies," *Vogue* (July 1989): 77.
33. Spike Lee, "Spike Lee Replies [to Joe Klein]," letter to the editor, *New York* (July 17, 1989): 2.
34. Loic Wacquant, "Redrawing the Urban Color Line: The State of the Ghetto in the 1980s," in *Social Problems,* Craig Calhoun and George Ritzer, eds. (New York: McGraw-Hill, 1992), pp. 448–75.
35. Mike Davis, *City of Quartz* (London: Verso, 1990), pp. 223–32.
36. Ibid., p.270.
37. Roncayolo, *La ville et ses territoires,* p. 212.
38. Charles V. Hamilton, *Adam Clayton Powell Jr.: The Political Biography of an American Dilemma* (New York: Athenaeum, 1991).

3 Polyphony and Cultural Expression

INTERPRETING MUSICAL TRADITIONS IN *DO THE RIGHT THING*

It has been generally accepted that classical Hollywood films incorporate music in order to construct and maintain an audience of passive consumers to whom the sound track is usually inaudible or invisible.[1] In this model, film music exists to enhance the purported and desired seamlessness of the narrative (for example by covering over edits). The conventional score is typically characterized by several elements, including a strong orientation to nineteenth-century European Romanticism, which prioritizes melody, lush sound, and full orchestration, and a frequent reliance on leitmotifs, which are variously associated with specific themes or characters. Music is used to orient and hook the spectator, from assisting in emphasizing visual cues to monitoring or manipulating physiological reactions to the film.

While studios of the 1950s promoted musicals as the ultimate fusion of new visual technologies and original aural spectacle in an attempt to reclaim the lost audience of the postwar years, the rock-and-roll films from the late 1950s on offered the same cinematic/sound feast, as well as a new appeal to the youth audience or teen demographic market. The 1960s saw the positioning of popular rock music as a site of political and ethnic expression, while the late 1960s and 1970s saw previously sub-cultural forms of music (e.g., punk, reggae, and rap) infiltrate mainstream entertainment, including popular cinema.

Recently, as initially black, urban musical forms such as hip hop and rap were incorporated into and appropriated by domi-nant culture, rap films began to show up on the commercial screen (e.g., *Boyz N the Hood, Juice,* and *Menace II Society*). With the late-twentieth-century proliferation of visual-aural media and media technology, audiences have to process and respond to an intermingling of video and audio phenomena on a level that exceeds classical, conventional film-music demands in the sheer amount of music involved and in the number of impli-cated musical traditions and references. (This is not to imply, however, that contemporary spectators are somehow more knowledgeable or sophisticated than past film audiences.)

MUSIC, HISTORY, AND THE FILMS OF SPIKE LEE

Spike Lee's "authorial" position regarding music and narrative is at once oppositional (voicing black history within a traditionally white industrial context) and mainstream (promot-ing familiar black artists for commercial reproduction and con-sumption on a mass scale). From *She's Gotta Have It* to *Malcolm X*, Lee's commercial film releases have been characterized by the use of multiple musical styles that connote black production, artistry, and history. While *School Daze* popularized "Da Butt" and used elaborate musical production numbers to debate "straight" versus "nappy," the chronicle of Bleek Gilliam's jazz career in *Mo' Better Blues* is overtly *about* music and performance. *Jungle Fever* uses several musical voices, although there is no overlap or intermingling among them: each musical tradition is assigned to a particular family of characters, while the film is dominated, overall, by Stevie Wonder's original songs. A bio-graphical epic, *Malcolm X* omits titles as markers of historical progress and instead indicates the passage of time through interludes of music by recognizable black artists such as Lionel Hampton and Billie Holliday (and – by the closing credits – Arrested Development).

Lee is clearly conversant in classical musical use and narrative conventions. Classical scoring and style, however, form only one voice within the multilayered text of *Do the Right Thing* (*DRT*). Here, Lee manipulates convention in a traditional manner to orient spectators within the film story. His expansion of traditional musical and visual expectations joins other musical traditions, such as jazz, radio, and rap, with camera movement and visual design to visibly depart from the classical idiom. While classical techniques are apparent in the film, the overall effect of Lee's layering is one of challenge to those expectations and to invisible style.

DRT arguably represents his most coherent use of music as interactive with and an essential component of visual representation and thematic, political concerns. The preexisting popular music (by groups such as Public Enemy and EU) and scored sound track of *DRT* work together in a process of continual clash and merger, not as discrete segments. Unlike the artists featured in *Jungle Fever* or *X*, Public Enemy and EU were known primarily within black, urban culture before the film's release – not as popular/mainstream. Finally, while *DRT* is not overtly about music or musicians, it is Lee's most thoroughly musical film – a film that posits rap music and rap style as commercially embraceable by the mainstream although inherently politically oppositional. For Lee, black musical production reflects black history and politics – through popular musical and aesthetic styles – which can be produced, marketed, and sold to a mass audience through cinema.

"RAP AESTHETIC" AND SPECTATORIAL ADDRESS

Before the opening title sequence of *DRT*, a solo tenor saxophone plays a mournful variation of "Lift Every Voice and

*clly —
illuse's
the
point*

Sing" over the symbol of Universal Pictures. The screen then goes black for a split second before a splash of hot red colors reveals a woman dancing vigorously, in several different street settings, to Public Enemy's "Fight the Power." While the backdrop and her bright spandex outfits change, the actress remains centrally framed, as all cuts are made on action. Although this sequence has been criticized for its apparently narratively unmotivated music-video-like style and its objectification of Rosie Perez,[2] it is extremely significant for its foregrounding of an immediate, equivalent, and co-dependent alliance between the film's visual image and the musical sound track.

The opening sequence introduces *DRT*'s rap aesthetic – a visual style that adopts the formal characteristics (including rapid cuts and shifts in framing, and references to multiple styles and genres from music video to direct cinema and from melodrama to documentary) and thematic concerns of rap music (especially as it is characterized by the "politicized" voice of black, urban males). The film continues to use nondiegetic and diegetic music together with ambient noise, silence, dialogue, and the visual image to create a play of competing and merging voices.[3] These voices, as in rap, "sample" or combine snatches of musical traditions that are historically and culturally associated with or coded as African-American forms such as blues and popular soul music. Dialogical voices are primarily those of young urban African-Americans. Here, even before the titles, and then during the titles but long before the narrative begins, an aural dialectic is at work: two black American musical traditions – historic jazz and contemporary rap – are juxtaposed within the same space.

DRT uses music unconventionally, or obtrusively, in order to complement its formal style and thematic concerns. The amount of music and blend of multiple musical styles are used in a near-assaultive manner in specific sequences of the film, purposely giving the overall viewing experience a quality of excess and spectatorial challenge similar to rap's rapid-fire address.

For example, the racial diversity of *DRT*'s Bed-Stuy setting is underscored as a group of Latino youth who are gathered on a stoop endure the heat and the sounds of the streets around them with the help of a radio which broadcasts a salsa beat. The group is briefly energized when it engages in an all-out battle of bass and volume with the strolling Radio Raheem, a black youth whose boom box drowns out the salsa with Public Enemy. While Raheem disposes of the aural competition quickly, the scene's overall layering of ambient sound, the group's radio, and Raheem's rap, combined with vibrant colors, camera angles, and edits, creates an ongoing aural-visual dialectic that suggests a rap aesthetic. The significance of Radio Raheem's boom box and the accompanying use of Public Enemy's "Fight the Power" will be discussed in detail later.

DRT's provision of space for the expression and competition of multiple ethnic and generational voices – although they are predominantly male – denies the emergence of any singular empowered voice. Potentially, then, the film is a "space of the vocal (oral ethnography, people's history, slave narratives) . . . way(s) of restoring voice to the silenced" – a description that also defines the terrain and aspiration of much rap expression.[4] Even if *DRT*'s aims and accomplishments are not so ideologically suggestive, the film issues a challenge to the classic spectator, who is conceived as passive and soothed by music of which she or he is unaware.

The dialogical dynamism implied by Spike Lee's use of diverse musical traditions suggests music's active engagement of an audience that may or may not be culturally fluent in the vocal play of these texts. While the film's music *could* be heard only musically (or not in terms of its cultural associations), its invocation of musical styles that are distinctly grounded in predominantly black cultural experience challenges the spectator to actively position her- or himself against or within those traditions – to be, in fact, overtly aware of the symbolically laden values of the music as a separate text in addition to its filmic-narrative value.

Lee's audience thus breaks down into knowing or informed readers who are culturally inscribed within or by the discursive power and social significance of particular musical styles, and other viewers who are challenged to become educated to an exchange of cultural voices that typically remain absent or silent from their sphere of cultural-ideological operation. Perplexed responses to the film's ending and the hypothetical space that the multiple-voiced text provides would seem to indicate the fragmented subjectivity which is promoted in *DRT*'s spectators, as continual negotiation of the different musical voices of the text is required in order to fully engage the narrative.[5] Ultimately, it might be asked whether *DRT*'s musical address calls for a new type of spectatorship or a reworking of classical cinematic reception away from a model of passive consumption toward a conception of active negotiation of preexistingly familiar (aural) texts, couched in an original (visual) context.[6]

I will argue here that close analysis of *DRT*'s "polyphonic" approach to aural content – as it is coordinated with visual style – explains and illustrates the significance of Lee's assertion that it is his "most political film."[7] However, this assertion is qualified by the fact that, for Lee, commercial popular cultural artifacts produced by Blacks – here, explicitly music (the word), but also fashion (the image) – are *inherently* political, as they emerge from a position marginalized by dominant control of capital and communication.

MUSICAL TRADITIONS IN *DO THE RIGHT THING*

Two distinct musical traditions are employed to create symbolic meaning via their place in *DRT*'s particular social-historical, cultural context. The first of these traditions is a romantic, American folk-inflected orchestral style that also incorporates jazz, blues music, and instrumentation. Because of its thematic use in the film and by virtue of its mediated nature (Coplandesque orchestral to bluesy jazz combo), this tradition can be referred to as "historic-nostalgic." The historic-nostalgic tradition is embodied in the original sound-track music scored for the film by William Lee, the director's father. It serves primarily as background music or underscoring but at some points it intersects with the second tradition – of contemporary, popular commercial music. This second tradition has two modes of expression within the film: rap music ("Fight the Power") – which is played continuously by Radio Raheem – and the soul and R&B records played by Mister Señor Love Daddy, a disc jockey on the neighborhood radio station, We Love Radio 108 FM.

For the most part, both the rap and soul strains of the contemporary-commercial tradition exist strictly as diegetic music, although there are scenes in which the music carries over from another context in which it is not explicitly visually linked to the apparatus producing the music. Part of the narrative significance of the film's source music is tied to the fact that all the songs have lyrics, some of which are more significant and audible than others. Love Daddy also presents a dialogic patter that flows in and out of and bridges these lyrical texts. The film employs the historic-nostalgic tradition and the commercial-contemporary tradition to delineate geographic space (a block in the largely black urban neighborhood of Bedford-Stuyvesant in Brooklyn) and historical moment (i.e., the topicality of the subject matter and theme, in this space of race relations between African-Americans, Italian-Americans, Koreans, and Latinos) and to clarify characterization (both of and within urban black culture and generationally).

THE HISTORIC-NOSTALGIC TRADITION

Universal Studio's press information that anticipated *DRT*'s release described composer William Lee as "the noted bassist, composer and arranger of eight folkjazz operas."[8] Folkjazz is probably the best description of Bill Lee's background music, which is included in almost 30 minutes of the 120-minute film. His nondiegetic score, structured by conventional folk and more unconventional jazz strains (ranging from low-key bluesy solos to virtual funk explosions), assists in *DRT*'s

FIGURE 7

Sal lectures an unrepentant Mookie. (Courtesy of the Museum of Modern Art, New York.)

complex interweaving of communal aspirations and ideals with the clash of generational and individual aspirations and intolerances.

While the stringy folk inflections complement the sense of history and togetherness felt by the residents of the block and suggest the time-tested wisdom of Mother Sister and Da Mayor's generation by repeatedly associating with them, the jazz strains, often associated with Mookie and Sal, suggest the active, contemporary, struggling, and unresolved voices of this polyphonic work. As Marshall Stearns has noted, jazz, as a musical and cultural voice, is "distinguished by an immediacy of communication, an expressiveness characteristic of the free use of the human voice . . . European harmony, Euro-African melody, and African rhythm."[9] The folk-orchestral and the African-American musical traditions of jazz represent voices that are, respectively and symbolically, one of status quo and nostalgic association (aligned with assimilation, passivity, and social acceptance) and one of continual resistance and assertiveness (aligned with exceptionalism, activity, and social change).

Composed for Bill Lee's Natural Spiritual Orchestra, the score's instrumentation places heavy emphasis on multiple strings, which is what most clearly lends it its folk tone. The Copland-esque composition of these underscored segments is evocative of such value-laden symbols as heritage, neighborhood, and community – reflective of a block that is, on the surface, a unified place. This sense of stability is reinforced by the composition's strict adherence to classic cinema conventions for background music, including the maintenance of mezzo-forte dynamics, an emphasis on tonal, resolving harmonic patterns and melody, and unobtrusive instrumental entrances and exits in which the musical line elides gently into the next scene or resolves to a quiet, dominant chord that fades imperceptibly into an edit.

The folk-style idiom exists, visually, in the streets or as a component of the community that integrates the spectator into the Bed-Stuy universe. It is used to introduce the neighborhood characters: Smiley, a young adult with cerebral palsy who preaches the words of Malcolm X; Sal Frangione, the owner of Sal's Famous Pizzeria, and his sons; and Mother Sister and Da Mayor, the literal and symbolic old guard of the block who have seen its history and are wary of its future.

There are at least sixteen significant occurrences of historic-nostalgic themes in the film. Two of these are associated with two of the film's primary characters, Mookie and Sal. Four out of five times, Mookie's theme is heard when he is outside his workplace (Sal's Famous Pizzeria) – traversing the neighborhood on pizza delivery runs that require the camera to follow along, thus capturing the block's constant activity. This theme underscores

FIGURE 8
Sal and his sons, Vito (Richard Edson, on Sal's left) and Pino (John Turturro). (Courtesy of the Museum of Modern Art, New York.)

Spike Lee's recurring concern with older and younger genera-
tions, their knowledge, histories, and differing responses to contemporary problems of race relations. It is present, for example,
as Mookie acknowledges Mother Sister, the eyes and ears of the
block from the older generation, and Mister Señor Love Daddy,
who represents the middle generation. Sal's theme is associated
with his pizzeria and his family, their history, and their current
struggles as a Bed-Stuy business. These musical motifs establish a
crucial theme regarding the interconnectedness of private lives
and public space, or the inability of individuals to escape the
neighborhood's gaze and judgment of private actions.

The historic-nostalgic score implies here that an idyllic community is realizable. Such a community takes heed of the knowledge of its elders and embraces the present with youthful enthu-
siasm. These themes are introduced in moments of placidity
and neighborhood communication or in the context of family
relationships and a discussion of social issues. Each occurrence is
tied to expressions of the neighborhood's closeness as a commu-

nity with an extensive history of people who know and literally watch over one another. These unifying themes are supported by the use of long tracking shots that enable visualization of the entire block (from within Sal's and outside) and establish the locus of the film's action.

JAZZ, HEAT, AND RACE

DRT's characters, however, also struggle with ever-present prejudices and biases of and toward those who are not like them (the Korean market owners and, eventually, Sal and his sons) or who are somehow separable from the community. If the string-orchestral strains of music suggest a communal ideal, jazz strains in the score hint at a barely repressed undercurrent of turbulence and unrest, and imply the tremendous frustrations and simmering threat of violence.

The second entrance of Sal's theme, for example, is set in a tense environment, in which Sal and Pino, his openly racist son, discuss the future of the pizzeria in Bed-Stuy as opposed to their home turf of Italian-American Bensonhurst. Pino becomes increasingly frustrated and violently animated, asserting his disgust with his life and surroundings. Sal, on the other hand, grows increasingly dejected in the face of such anger directed at his life's work. The neighborhood voices interjected here are those of the "corner men" – who sit on the street corner all Saturday, commenting on local activity – and Smiley, who approaches Pino and Sal and tries to sell photographs of African-American political leaders.

The music in this sequence enters with a solemn, slowly descending piano line. This same melody is later picked up by a violin, then a cello, a soprano sax, and a group of violins. Next, with a strong undercurrent of strings and ascending piano chords, the jazz section emerges. A solo soprano saxophone accompanied by a piano and trap set launches, with increasing intensity and higher pitch, into fevered improvisational runs.

FIGURE 9
Pino kneading his dough. A frustrated single white man strokes his livelihood. (Courtesy of the Museum of Modern Art, New York.)

Visually, Sal and Pino's scene is matched with the music in intensity and color. The sequence begins with a slow tracking shot from the back wall of the pizzeria to a two-shot of Sal and Pino, who sit at a front table. The opening track matches the slow piano scale and settles into a relatively static two-shot as both come to rest. From inside Sal's, however, external action is visible and takes place on several planes. The neighborhood is, in fact, ever-present and ever-visible (and, equally, ever-watchful of the pizzeria). The layered pieces of the jazz combo and the improvisation in this particular scene, then, act as companions to the action that confronts Pino and Sal from the outside and in some ways pries them apart, anticipating the tragic events to come.

Spike Lee wanted the visual design of his film to "look hot. . . . The audience should feel like it's suffocating."[10] The improvisational interludes Branford Marsalis interjects into folk-jazz sequences elaborate upon and intensify this effect. These passages evoke a fevered, aggravated play with chromatic intervals that translates into a sense of struggle and a lack of harmonic expression. In Sal and Pino's scene, then, instrumental underscoring palpably matches the mood of the characters and informs the gravity of their actions. The transition from the mournful piano and strings associated with Sal's introspection to the aggressive, reedy soprano saxophone solo, which rises and explodes with Pino's enraged outburst (significantly, taken out on Smiley in his latest halting attempt to literally sell the irreconcilable images and messages of Malcolm X and Martin Luther King, Jr.), ruptures the surface calm of the neighborhood's status quo.

RAP STYLE: "IN-YOUR-FACE EXPLOSIVE"

As Tricia Rose's discussions of rap note, it is a musical style that is representative of both resistance and mediation. The "tension between rap's confining rhythmic patterns and its aggressive presentation potentially assaults," and the "end of the song brings relief" – especially for the white middle-class listener, who may feel threatened by rap's lyric and percussive demands. Rap is a "complex fusion of folk orality and postmodern technology," a form whose style and substance consist of compromise.[11]

If instrumental music expresses that which is not verbalizable in culture, then rap is made even more potentially threatening by its basis in verbalization or "the word."[12] Rap is an increasingly popular commercial musical form for which "melody is clearly secondary to the primary interest. . . . [its] songs . . . are incantations, chants which can correctly be seen as thematic variations on the question of power, racism, class."[13] Because of

FIGURE 10
Radio Raheem (Bill Nunn) patrols with his ghetto blaster in hand.
(Courtesy of the Museum of Modern Art, New York.)

Western culture's proclivity to binarism and the polarization of spoken language and singing, rap's dialogic, rhythmic, linguistic structure, combined with its sampling of everything from former pop hits to television theme songs (or its pastiche form and overt political message and intent), renders it potentially disjunctive amid conventional musical forms.

Lee's choice of rap in *DRT* as an inescapable diegetic element emphasizes his expressed political concerns and focus. His use of the rap music of Public Enemy presents a challenge to convention by insisting on spectator attention to its consuming presence, which drowns out any competing dialogue and seems to guide framing and camera movement. The rap qualities determine the filmic.

DRT uses "Fight the Power" in ten scenes, including the opening titles. Except in the title sequence, "Fight" serves as the personal anthem of Radio Raheem, who is visually and dialogically constructed as strong, quiet, and commanding. Generally, "Fight" is heard from offscreen, immediately before Raheem appears. Visually, Lee enhances the notion that Raheem and rap are physically powerful and aurally threatening by using sweeping camera movements that start with Raheem's gargantuan boom box – exaggerated in close-up – and travel rapidly up his body to reveal his massive frame. Raheem is usually shot with the camera in a canted position and from a low angle, almost mimicking the position of the boom box itself and suggesting that the aural barrage of "Fight" sets things askew and ensures Raheem's/rap's dominance of any given scene. The song is used as a sonic assault – it enters unpredictably, at an unmodulated, uncharacteristically loud volume. It is intended to be obtrusive.

The aural explosion created by "Fight," reinforced by Lee's exaggerated camera angles, suggests that rap is a potentially totalizing aesthetic system. In the presence of "the word," one's worldview (via Lee's camera lens) is altered – or at least made alterable. Rap's association with the youthful Raheem, its aggressive political message (here), and its capacity to set the entire neighborhood at attention (aurally and spatially) imply that his generation of black youth is allied with change, in contrast to Mother Sister and Da Mayor's accommodationist stances. Significantly, however, Raheem himself is almost entirely silent. He does not speak the language of rap; he is "spoken by" it. Communication, for Raheem, is enacted by both the aural dominance of rap and the visual symbols of hip-hop culture. Raheem's knuckle rings and Nikes are part of a network of consumer goods that displace individual expression and re-present it via shorthand material markers that are both representable to and understandable across a generalized social field (e.g., as connoting contemporary American, urban, black, male youth, whether or not worn exclusively by such individuals). (In the next chapter, Douglas Kellner analyzes *DRT*'s representation of urban black style as a form of cultural politics.)

It should be noted, however, that one of *DRT*'s methods for promoting audience sympathy for Raheem and portraying the senselessness of his death is to gradually render Public Enemy's tract familiar via its repetition. Overall, the spatial (noise pollution, because of its unmodulated volume and its encroachment on silent space) and the verbal (politicized lyrics, in comparison with the surrounding environment: that which speaks the unspeakable) content of the song are, finally, rendered relatively nonconfrontational. This familiarity, significantly, allows for the sale of Public Enemy's music outside the film – as featured on the sound-track album. Its nonthreatening status is, equally, narratively conferred upon Radio Raheem, whose literal lack of voice throughout the film enables his image, or iconographic status within the neighborhood, to supersede his individual persona and, thereby, promotes the film's heroization of the youth at the close of the narrative and into the end credits.

"You come into Sal's, there's no music. No rap, no music, no music, no music. Capisc'? Understand?"
(Sal to Radio Raheem in *DRT*)

While "music can act on the body" and thus trigger emotional responses "through its rhythm (speed and emphasis of beat), its dynamics (loudness or softness) and its pitch (high or low),"[14] Lee uses overlapping dialogue and ambient sound, which frequently share these characteristics, to play "musical" roles. Sal's Famous Pizzeria is unique in *DRT* because it is such a quiet site. On the six occasions in which music is used in Sal's, two are the unwelcome rap intrusions made by Raheem, three include entrances from or exits to the street – thus incorporating the neighborhood/external context – and two of these sequences are explicitly associated with Mookie's theme. Sal's "no music" assertion is, therefore, one that holds fast. In the pizzeria, expressions of racial and class differences or discussions of sociocultural conflicts are suppressed. Buggin' Out is thrown out for asking that there be "brothers up on this Wall of Fame . . . Malcolm X, Angela Davis, Michael Jordan," who would reflect Sal's clientele and its interests, as opposed to the photos of Italian-American celebrities. Sal's prominent display of Frank Sinatra's photograph, in particular, references a musical voice that is not aurally present but that is nonetheless visually and socially perceptible, thus contributing to the text's web of dialogical voices, voices that are portrayed as inadequate or even obsolete in contemporary urban America. Radio Raheem's Public Enemy not only imposes music upon Sal's space but infuses the popular neighborhood hangout with unwelcome social criticism from a young, urban, black male perspective:

> While the black man's sweatin'
> In the rhythm I'm rollin'
> Got to give us what we want
> Got to give us what we need
> Our freedom of speech is the freedom of death
> We got to fight the powers that be
> To revolutionize make a change
> What we need is awareness
> Power to the people, no delay.[15]

When Raheem first enters Sal's, he is shot from a low angle; Sal, behind the counter, is shot from above. Wide-angle lenses flatten Sal into his wall, while Radio Raheem's face is distorted and becomes ominously large and looming. These visual power relations are enhanced by the use of canted framing. Once Raheem voluntarily turns his music off – after Sal's screaming appeals (his world will not be challenged or altered by "that noise") – shots are framed from a neutral angle, at medium- to long-shot distance. Visually and aurally, Raheem's music brings the current of tension at Sal's into the open.

In his final entrance into the pizzeria Raheem is accompanied by Buggin' Out and Smiley as they come to inform Sal of their boycott. The sound of the boom box precedes their entrance, which is again accompanied by a canted frame and shot from a low angle. As tensions rise in the scene and Sal breaks down to screaming racist invectives, he "kills" Radio Raheem's box by smashing it repeatedly with a baseball bat. From this point through the ensuing killing of Raheem and destruction of Sal's – a time span of approximately twelve film minutes – there is no music on the sound track, only ambient noise and sound effects. The "silence" of the sound track (although it is filled with crowd noise) would seem to enhance – especially in light of the historic-nostalgic tradition's function – the film's tone of complete chaos and social breakdown. The cinematic spectator is cast in a participatory role by virtue of the absence of any music that would soothe the tension and violence. The audience is thus set on the same psychological plane as those observing or participating in the uprising, by hearing only what they hear. Without any voice to comment on the action, the spectator's identification is set adrift.

CONTEMPORARY SOUL RADIO

If the historic-nostalgic and rap styles of music ostensibly represent opposite poles of convention, then Mister Señor Love Daddy's neighborhood radio station appears to serve as a bridge between the two, both aurally with regard to genre and generationally with regard to characterization. In accord with Eisler's and Adorno's idea that "music bears the sociological/ psychological value of evoking the collective community," the radio station's "social function is that of a cement, which holds together elements that otherwise would oppose each other unrelated. . . . It binds" neighborhood inhabitants together "into a community of listener-participants."[16]

The station is an organizing voice for the neighborhood because of the disc jockey's on-air narrative patter. Mister Señor Love Daddy's linguistic authority, together with the mixture of recorded music he plays, forges a loose connection with Radio Raheem's rap. Love Daddy's talk and his records also parallel the folk-jazz idiom in bridging edits and evoking a harmonious neighborhood environment.[17] His voice and music, emanating from each available source on the block, suggest his position as a mediator among polyphonically voiced audiences.

The contemporary selections the radio station plays reflect 108 FM's diverse neighborhood audience, from the a cappella of Take 6, the dance music of EU, and the ballads of Al Jarreau and Perry Como to the salsa of Ruben Blades and the reggae of Steel Pulse. Thematically, apart from the suggestion that Love Daddy's omnipresence establishes the radio station as an object of communal understanding and discourse, 108 FM serves an educational function. While Love Daddy voices his dismay over the racial differences and inanities that led to violence ("My people, my people. What can I say? Say what I can. . . . Are we gonna live together? Together are we gonna live?"), he equally heralds the richness of black culture in a rhythmic salute to a potential Wall of Fame for the community to truly call its own. This "roll call" is a voiced poetic collection of names such as Mahalia Jackson, Duke Ellington, Anita Baker, and Aretha Franklin, underscored by the folk-jazz music of William Lee. (Notably, most of these artists are Motown recording artists, thus referencing Berry Gordy's black-owned-and-operated business, artistic success, and "family" work ethos, as well as indirectly advertising the sound-track album, which was produced on the Motown label.) The roll call is visually matched with a montage of the neighborhood's history, its old-timers, Mother Sister, Da Mayor, the corner men, and the patrolling police. Thematically, Love Daddy's dialogue here connects black cultural heritage and pride with the neighborhood's cultural heritage and pride. Lee positions Bed-Stuy as a microcosm of contemporary African-American culture.[18]

DRT concludes with end titles that are introduced by Love Daddy's dedication of an orchestral piece to Radio Raheem that elides into the (recognized unofficial black national) anthem, "Lift Every Voice and Sing." Lee's presentation of balancing quotes by Martin Luther King, Jr., and Malcolm X parallels the opening credit sequence in the critical attacks and confusion it has drawn. Within the logic of the competing musical voices throughout the film, however, the quotations reinforce *DRT* as a text of purposefully, unresolvably conflicting voices, each with committed desires and goals. King discusses the value of an integrated community of "brotherhood" in "dialogue" – an ethos that is symbolized in the film by orchestral themes and the older generation that holds the unity of the block/neighborhood family as the highest good. Malcolm X speaks to individual suffering and disparities (the experiences shared by the community but felt differently by each person) in terms of the advocacy of violence in self-defense – an address that is acutely relevant to the young generation in Bed-Stuy, for whom dialogue has failed (Sal and Raheem literally do not speak the same language) and physical action is the only response left.

SPECTATORSHIP AND COMMODITY PRACTICE

DRT's indulgence in a rap aesthetic implies that the film threatens to reconstruct or to expressly confront the cinematic spectator with her or his act of listening/viewing and her or his reaction to the text. The fundamental aurality of *DRT* combined with its hot look and camera movements conspires to create an address that is perhaps much further in its operation from cinematic suturing than it is similar to the affective, physiological response generally attributed to music *as* music and perhaps most provocative of further study – to the interpellative strategies of television as an "ongoing video collage."[19]

Certainly, Spike Lee's background in commercial and music video production often provides an opening for a predictably traditional criticism of his films which suggests that his work has more "in common with Madonna than with Malcolm X."[20] Lee's "politicized" voice is most conflicted – in its calls for immediate racial and economic representation, recognition, challenge, and change – as his films grant expression to voices that are typically marginalized in relation to the mainstream, only for those oppositions to be subsumed by larger commodification practices that recoup them for popular sale as black history and politics. Perhaps in spite of themselves, however, Lee's films may represent a provocative, positive fusion of a prolific, chameleon-like visual-aural aesthetic – a fusion that incorporates diverse youth concerns (in terms of response rather than generational affiliation) and plays with spectator activity and popular knowledge in an unprecedented fashion.

NOTES

This essay is a slightly revised version of an article that originally appeared in *Film Quarterly* 47:2 (Winter 1993–94): 18–29. The author would like to thank David James, Marsha Kinder, and Kathryn Kalinak for their comments and discussions.

1. Claudia Gorbman, *Unheard Melodies: Narrative Film Music* (Bloomington: Indiana University Press, 1987), pp. 58, 75. Gorbman refers to "untroublesome viewing subjects." "Film music" here includes both nondiegetic and diegetic music. Nondiegetic music – or what is conventionally conceived of as "sound-track music" – is, Gorbman notes, that which is typically meant to be invisible. Diegetic music is audible to the characters within the film.
2. Stanley Crouch, "Do the Race Thing: Spike Lee's Afro-Fascist Chic," *Village Voice* (June 20, 1989). See, especially, descriptions of Lee's "luster of surface brilliance" and "turning of people into things."

(Probably the most interesting black feminist reading of this opening scene is formulated by bell hooks in "Counter-Hegemonic Art:
Do the Right Thing," in her book of essays *Yearning: Race, Gender
and Cultural Politics* [Boston: South End Press, 1990].)

3. Robert Stam, "Bakhtin, Polyphony and Ethnic/Racial Representation," in *Unspeakable Images: Ethnicity and the American Cinema*, ed.
Lester Friedman (Champaign-Urbana: University of Illinois Press,
1991), p. 262.

4. Ibid., p. 256.

5. See, for example, David Denby, "He's Gotta Have It," *New York*
(June 26, 1989): 53–54.

6. Lee's films in general would seem to support such an inquiry. I
would argue that many films of the "New Black Hollywood" movement of the 1980s and 1990s challenge traditional subjectivity
aesthetically and through aural content and style.

7. Spike Lee with Lisa Jones, *Do the Right Thing: A Spike Lee Joint* (New
York: Simon & Schuster, 1989), p. 21.

8. Universal News Press Release, 1989.

9. Quoted in Simon Frith, *Sound Effects* (New York: Pantheon, 1981),
p. 16.

10. Lee with Jones, *Do the Right Thing*, p. 2.

11. Tricia Rose, "Orality and Technology: Rap Music and Afro-
American Cultural Resistance," *Popular Music and Society* 13:4
(1989): 37, 38. The phrase "in-your-face explosive" is from Kenneth
Turan, "Lee's Fury in Control in *Fever*," *Los Angeles Times* (June 7,
1991), p. F19, Turan's assessment of *Do the Right Thing* as contrasted
with *Jungle Fever*.

12. Ray Jackendoff, *Consciousness and the Computational Mind* (Cambridge, MA: MIT Press, 1987).

13. Wheeler Winston Dixon, "Urban Black American Music in the Late
1980s: The 'Word' as Cultural Signifier," *Midwest Quarterly* 30:2
(Winter 1989): 229.

14. William Johnson, "Face the Music," *Film Quarterly* 22:4 (Summer
1969): 3.

15. Public Enemy, "Fight the Power," Def Jam Records, Inc. (CBS,
1989).

16. Gorbman, *Unheard Melodies*, p. 40.

17. Stam, "Bakhtin, Polyphony," p. 25. As Stam notes, while the "visual
organization of space . . . is a metaphor of exclusions and hierarchi-
cal arrangements . . . the concept of voice," and, by extension,
music, "suggests a metaphor of seepage across boundaries which
. . . redefines spatiality itself."

18. Portia Maultsby, "Soul Music: Its Sociological and Political Significance in American Popular Culture," *Journal of Popular Culture* 17 (Fall 1983): 54.

19. Jon Pareles, "How Rap Moves to Television's Beat," *New York Times* (January 14, 1990), Section 2, p. 28.

20. Bernadette D. Soter, "Letter to Editor," *Los Angeles Times* (June 7, 1991), Calendar, p. 79.

4 Aesthetics, Ethics, and Politics in the Films of Spike Lee

During the 1980s, Hollywood joined Ronald Reagan and his administration in neglecting African-American issues and concerns.[1] Few serious films during the decade featured Blacks; instead, Blacks were generally stereotypically portrayed in comedies, often with an African-American comic like Richard Pryor or Eddie Murphy playing against a white buddy.[2] In this context, Spike Lee's films constitute a significant intervention into the Hollywood film system. Addressing issues of race, gender, and class from a resolutely black perspective, Lee's films provide insights into these explosive problematics missing from mainstream white cinema. Starting with low-budget independent pictures like *Joe's Bed-Stuy Barbershop: We Cut Heads* and *She's Gotta Have It,* Lee moved to Hollywood financing of his films starting with *School Daze,* a focus on black college life that spoofed the college film genre and the musical. His next film, *Do the Right Thing (DRT),* was immediately recognized as an important cinematic statement concerning the situation of Blacks in contemporary U.S. society, and the films that followed (*Mo' Better Blues, Jungle Fever, Malcolm X,* and *Crooklyn*) won Lee recognition as one of the most important filmmakers at work in the United States today.

73

Moreover, Lee's financial and critical successes helped open the door to more studio-produced and -distributed black-directed films. The profits made by Lee's films showed that there was an audience for black films dealing with contemporary realities. Estimates suggest that from 25 to 30 percent of the U.S. film audience is African-American (overrepresenting Blacks' 13 percent of the population), and Hollywood calculated that there was a significant audience for black-oriented films.[3] Moreover, the profits from Lee's early low-budget films procured continued financing of his own films and paved the way for a renaissance of films by (usually young male) African-Americans during the 1990s.[4]

In this essay, I examine Spike Lee's aesthetics, vision of morality, and politics, arguing that his aesthetic strategies draw on Brechtian modernism and that his films are morality tales that convey ethical images and messages to their audiences. I also discuss Lee's politics, focusing on the figure of Malcolm X in Lee's work and his sometimes contradictory identity politics, in which politics per se are subordinate to creating one's identity and identity is defined primarily in terms of cultural style. Despite their limitations, Lee's films address key issues of race, gender, sexuality, class, and black politics. Cumulatively, they provide a compelling cinematic exploration of the situation of Blacks in contemporary U.S. society and of the limited political options at their disposal. I begin with a reading of *DRT*, turn to *Malcolm X* (hereafter in this essay *X*), and conclude with more general comments on Lee's gender politics, identity politics, and aesthetic strategies.[5]

DO THE RIGHT THING AS A BRECHTIAN MORALITY TALE

DRT takes place in a Brooklyn ghetto on the hottest day of the year. Mookie (played by Spike Lee) gets up and goes to work at Sal's Famous Pizzeria on a Saturday morning. Various neighborhood characters appear as Lee paints a tableau of the interactions between Blacks and Italians and the Hispanic and Korean residents of the Brooklyn ghetto of "Bed-Stuy." Conflicts between the Blacks and Italians erupt, and when a black youth is killed by the police, the crowd destroys the pizzeria.

Lee set out to make a film about black urban experience from a black perspective. His film transcodes the discourses, style, and conventions of African-American culture, with an emphasis on black nationalism that affirms the specificity of black experience and its differences from mainstream white culture. Lee presents black ways of speaking, walking, dressing, and acting, drawing on black slang, music, images, and style. His films are richly textured ethnographies of urban Blacks negotiating the allures of the consumer and media society and the dangers of racism and an oppressive urban environment. The result is a body of work that represents uniquely black perspectives, voices, styles, and politics.

Yet Lee also draws on the techniques of modernism and produces original innovative films that articulate his own vision and aesthetic style. In particular, like the German artist Bertolt Brecht, Spike Lee dramatizes the necessity of making moral and political choices.[6] Both Brecht and Lee produce a sort of "epic drama" that paints a wide tableau of typical social characters, shows examples of social and asocial behavior, and delivers didactic messages to the audience. Both Brecht and Lee utilize music, comedy, drama, vignettes of typical behavior, and figures who present the messages the author wishes to convey. Both present didactic learning plays, which strive to teach people to discover and then do "the right thing," while criticizing improper and antisocial behavior. Brecht's plays (as well as his prose, his film *Kuhle Wampe,* and his radio plays) depict character types in situations that force one to observe the consequences of typical behavior. Lee, I would argue, does the same thing in *DRT* (and most of his other films). In particular, the three street-corner philosophers, who offer comic commentary throughout, are very Brechtian, as is the radio disc jockey Mister Señor Love Daddy, who not only tells the audience to do the right thing throughout the movie ("and that's the truth, Ruth"), but repeatedly specifies "the right thing," insisting that the ghetto population "Wake up," "Love one another," and "Chill!"

DRT poses the question of political and social morality for its audience in the contemporary era: what is "the right thing" for oppressed groups like urban Blacks? The film is arguably modernist in that it leaves unanswered the question of the politically "right thing" to do. By "modernist," I refer, first, to aesthetic strategies of producing texts that are open and polyvocal, that disseminate a wealth of meanings rather than a central univocal meaning or message, and that require an active reader to produce the meanings.[7] Second, I take modernism to be an aesthetic tendency to produce unique works of art that bear the vision and stylistic imprint of their creator. Third, the type of modernism associated with what Peter Burger calls the "historical avant-garde" attempts to produce serious works that change individuals' perceptions and lives and strive to promote social transformation. Such movements as futurism, expressionism, Dadaism, and surrealism meet these criteria, as do the works of Brecht and Lee, though I ultimately argue that Lee's films contain a unique mixture of American popular cultural forms and modernism, inflected by Lee's African-American experience.[8]

I am claiming that in a formal sense the works of Spike Lee are in accord with these modernist criteria and that his aesthetic strategies are especially close to those of Brecht. Lee's texts tend to be open, to elicit divergent readings, and to generate a wealth of often divergent responses. He is, in this sense, an "auteur" whose films project a distinctive style and vision and comprise a coherent body of work with distinctive features. His work is highly serious and strives for specific transformative moral and political effects. Yet there are also ambiguities in Lee's work. While Mister Señor Love Daddy serves as a voice of social morality (*Sittlichkeit,* how to treat others) in *DRT,* it is an open question what, if any, political position Lee is affirming. Does he agree with the politics of Malcolm X or with those of Martin Luther King, Jr.? Is he advocating reform or revolution, integration or black nationalism, or a synthesis of the two?

Throughout the film, Public Enemy's powerful rap song "Fight the Power" resonates, but it is not clear from the film *how* one is supposed to fight the power or what political strategies one should employ to carry out the struggle. Indeed, one could read *DRT* as a postmodern evacuation of viable political options for Blacks and people of color in the present age.[9] That is, one could read the film as demonstrating that, politically, there is no "right thing" to do in the face of hopeless ghetto poverty, virulent racism, and a lack of viable political options and movements. In this postmodern reading, the film projects a bleak, nihilistic view of the future, marked by hopelessness and the collapse of modern black politics. In this context, political reformism and Martin Luther King's nonviolence appear to be questionable instruments of change. But it is not clear that violence is an attractive option, and one could even read the film as questioning social violence, by demonstrating that it ultimately hurts the people in the neighborhoods in which it explodes. (One could interpret the May 1992 Los Angeles uprising, which Lee's film uncannily anticipates, in a similar light.)

On this postmodern reading, it is not clear what the power is that one is supposed to fight, what instruments one is supposed to use, and what one's goals are supposed to be. This nihilistic interpretation suggests that modern politics as a whole are bankrupt,[10] that neither reform nor revolution can work, that African-Americans are condemned to hopeless poverty and the subordinate position of an oppressed underclass without the faintest possibility of improving their situation. Yet one could also read *DRT* as a modernist film that forces the viewer to compare the politics of Malcolm X and Martin Luther King and to decide for him- or herself what the "right thing" is for Blacks. In the following analysis, I examine whether *DRT* is a modernist or postmodernist film in both its style and politics, and whether Lee privileges Malcolm X or Martin Luther King in the film. But first I want to interrogate the cultural politics of *DRT*.

CULTURAL POLITICS IN *DO THE RIGHT THING*

The characters in *DRT* represent distinctive neighborhood African-, Hispanic-, Italian-, Anglo-, and Korean-American individuals, and Lee depicts their behavior and their conflicts with one another. Race he presents in terms of cultural identity and image, especially cultural style. Norman Denzin, in *Images of Postmodern Society*, argues that the characters wear T-shirts to identify their cultural politics and style.[11] For example, Mookie, the black worker in Sal's pizzeria, wears a Jackie Robinson baseball jersey, symbolizing a Black who breaks the color line in the white man's world (as Lee himself has done). While working, Mookie also wears a shirt with his name on it and the logo of "Sal's Pizzeria," signifying his position between the two worlds. Radio Raheem, whose radio blasts out "Fight the Power," provoking the confrontation with Sal, wears a T-shirt proclaiming "Bed-Stuy or Die." This message identifies him as a figure who asserts black solidarity and rebellion to preserve the community.

T-shirts also project a color-coding symbolism: Pino, Sal's racist son, wears white, while Vito, the son who gets along with Blacks, wears a black T-shirt. Sal's clothes code him as the boss/worker who drives up to his pizzeria in a Cadillac, but he dons an apron to make the pizzas, indicating that he is a petit-bourgeois small businessman. Other shirts identify the wearer with white or black cultural heroes. A young white man who has just purchased a ghetto apartment wears a Larry Bird Boston Celtics jersey, while a young black man wears the Los Angeles Lakers jersey of Magic Johnson. The Hispanics wear sleeveless colored T-shirts, while the older black men wear sleeveless white T-shirts, conventional single-colored shirts, or go topless. Most of the young women wear tube tops, though Mookie's sister, Jade, sports designer clothes.

FIGURE 11

A stylish Mookie offers advice to Vito, Sal's confused son. (Courtesy of the Museum of Modern Art, New York.)

Clothes and fashion accoutrements depict the various characters' styles and identity. Buggin' Out, an angry young black youth, sports a yellow African kente shirt, wears a gold chain around his neck, and has a gold tooth. He also wears Nike Air Jordan shoes (which Lee himself promotes in commercials), and explodes with anger when the Celtic fan accidentally soils them. Radio Raheem wears the same type of shoes himself, and his ghetto blaster and rap music establish his cultural identity (he plays only Public Enemy). He also wears a set of gold brass knuckle rings, engraved with "love" and "hate," which supposedly represent the two sides of the sometimes gentle and sometimes violent Raheem.[12] Mookie too sports a gold tooth and earring, marking him as a participant in black urban cultural conventions.[13] The three black street-corner philosophers, discoursing on the current situation of Blacks, are casually dressed, while the alcoholic Da Mayor (Ossie Davis) wears old and dirty clothes, coding him as an example of failed black manhood.

Mother Sister (Ruby Dee) dresses conventionally and represents traditional matriarchal black values in her disapproval of Da Mayor and "shiftless" young Blacks.

In fact, *DRT* influenced fashion trends: "The summer of 1989 saw millions of young people wearing Mookie-style surfer baggies over Lycra bike shorts."[14] Subsequently, Spike Lee designed his own T-shirts and clothes and opened a fashion store in Brooklyn; he also produced and acted in commercials for Nike Air Jordan shoes. He thus not only depicts a society in which cultural identity is produced through style and consumption but contributes to this trend with both his films and his commercial activity.[15]

The ways that mass cultural images pervade style and fashion suggest that cultural identity is constituted in part by iconic images of ethnic cultural heroes, which are badges of identity and forces of division between the races. Sal has pictures of famous Italian-Americans on the wall of his pizzeria (his "Wall of Fame"), and Buggin' Out's demand that pictures of Blacks be put on the wall and Sal's vehement refusal to do so precipitate the attempted boycott and subsequent violence. A stuttering and perhaps mentally retarded young African-American male, Smiley, sells pictures of Malcolm and Martin,[16] who appear as icons of black politics, while graffiti contain references to Jesse Jackson and Al Sharpton, who constitute black political leaders as cultural heroes, like sports and music stars.

These scenes suggest how media culture provides the material for identity and how different subcultures appropriate different images. Identity is thus formed on a terrain of struggle in which individuals choose their own cultural meanings and style in a differential system that always involves the affirmation of some tokens of identity and the rejection of others. Social institutions individuate people with social security numbers, voter registration rolls, consumer lists, data bases, police and academic records, and so on, but creating one's individual identity means refusing to be defined by these determinations. More and more, it is the case that media culture provides resources that are appropriated by audiences to make meanings, to create identities, as when teenage girls use Madonna as a model, or Blacks emulate African-American cultural heroes, or aspiring yuppies look to professionals on television shows like *LA Law* for patterns of identity.

Identity is thus mediated by mass-produced images, and image and cultural style are becoming ever more central to the construction of individual identities. Media culture is replacing nationalism, religion, the family, and education as sources of identity. Nationalism provides powerful imaginary community and cultural identities; it also produces forms of media culture that act as surrogates for both individuals and groups.[17]

Media culture also provides modern morality tales that demonstrate right and wrong behavior, that show what to do and what not to do, that indicate what is or is not "the right thing." Media culture is thus an important new force of socialization, and it is one of the merits of *DRT* that it puts this process of identity creation on display in a way that shows how different identities are produced in opposition to each other and represent a terrain in which social conflicts are played out.

DRT reveals how cultural identity is also articulated through music and expressive styles. The black disc jockey and Radio Raheem play exclusively black music, while the Puerto Rican street teens play Spanish-inflected music. A scene in which Radio Raheem and the Puerto Ricans duel with each other with loud-playing radios signifies the cultural clash and divisions in the ghetto community. In addition, Sal provokes Radio Raheem by ordering him to "turn that jungle music off. We ain't in Africa," while Buggin' Out replies, "Why it gotta be about jungle music and Africa?"

Thus, different cultures use popular music to establish their cultural identities, and different styles of music divide the community. But it is racial epithets that most pungently articulate the social conflicts and tensions. At a key juncture in the film, in modernist and Brechtian fashion, Lee interrupts his narrative and has the characters look into the camera to spit out vicious racial slurs, with Mookie attacking the Italians ("Dago, Wop, Guinea, garlic breath, pizza slingin' spaghetti bender"). Pino, the racist son, replies to the camera, assaulting Blacks: "Gold chain wearin' fried chicken and biscuit eatin' monkey, ape, baboon, fast runnin', high jumpin', spear chuckin', basket ball dunkin' titso spade, take your fuckin' pizza and go back to Africa."

A Puerto Rican attacks Koreans in similar racial terms and the Korean grocer attacks Jews. This scene brilliantly shows the racial differences encoded in language, but tends to equate all modes of racism as logically equivalent, whereas one could argue that the institutional racism against Blacks is far more virulent than the variegated cultural racisms articulated and that Lee never really catches the reality of racism as part of a system of oppression.[18] From this perspective, society especially oppresses people of color: not only is there racism and racial hatred among all races and ethnics, but there is an unequal distribution of power and wealth in U.S. society, in which Blacks and people of color tend to suffer disproportionately from systemic racial and class oppression. Put otherwise, Lee does not appear to understand that capitalism is a system of oppression that exploits and oppresses its underclass, particularly people of color.

Lee presents racism in personal and individualist terms as hostility among members of different groups, thus failing to illuminate the causes and structures of racism. Moreover, the film denigrates political action, caricaturing collective action and the tactic of the economic boycott, which served the Civil Rights movement so well.[19]

In addition, Lee constantly celebrates consumerism, the object of much of the film's focus, rather than depicting how consumerism has come to organize ghetto existence. Much emphasis is placed on eating pizza, ice cream, and ice cones, drinking beer, and displaying consumer items. As I noted, to a large extent identity is constructed through clothes and style, and no one questions consumerist practices.

Yet Lee incisively shows how clothes, music, language, and style separate the various ethnic groups in his vision of a divided

FIGURE 12

Da Mayor (Ossie Davis), Sal and his sons, Vito and Pino. (From the editor's collection.)

ghetto. Such a situation is ripe for violence, and *DRT* anticipated the Los Angeles uprisings that erupted in May 1992 after a white jury acquitted the policemen who were videotaped viciously beating Rodney King. *DRT* is thus properly read as a cautionary tale warning what might happen if relations between the races continue to worsen.

Thus, along with its limitations, *DRT* has its insights and can be said to articulate some of the conditions that produce violence in the ghettos. The film is particularly strong in depicting the explosion that erupts after Radio Raheem is killed by white policemen. Lee's own character, Mookie, throws a garbage can through the window of Sal's pizzeria and violence breaks out that destroys the establishment. A close viewing of Mookie's action suggests that it is a deliberate act and that Lee *is* presenting it as "the right thing." The camera zooms in on Mookie deliberating about what to do after the police have accidentally choked Radio Raheem to death in a fight that began when Sal smashed his beloved radio. Lee then pans a long and slow shot of Mookie methodically walking away to pick up a garbage can and then returning to throw it through the window of the pizzeria. Clearly he does it out of rage over Radio Raheem's death.[20] On this reading, Lee is privileging human life over property and is suggesting that violence against property is a legitimate act of retaliation. One could also argue that Mookie is directing the mob's violence against the pizzeria and away from Sal and his sons, thus ultimately protecting them from the mob's wrath.[21] It is, of course, debatable whether the act of violence was "the right thing," though it is a rejection of King's philosophy of nonviolence. And it is not clear whether this act produces anything positive for Mookie or the black community; one could indeed argue the opposite.[22] Smiley puts a picture of Malcolm X and Martin Luther King standing side by side on the wall, thus fulfilling Raheem's desire to have black images in the pizzeria. But the picture is then shown burning, raising the question of whether this represents the futility of black politics in the present age and allegorically enacts the fading relevance of both Malcolm and Martin.

In any case, the charge leveled by (white conservative) critics that *DRT* would lead to violence and increase race hatred is misplaced. Rather, Lee's film explores the social environment and racial tensions and conflicts that are likely to produce racial and other forms of urban violence. In interviews after the film was released, Lee protested that he was only depicting existing urban conditions and not offering solutions, and this position seems wholly reasonable.

Yet one could criticize Lee for deconstructing modern politics as futile or irrelevant, thus giving voice to a postmodern nihilism.[23] However, certain aspects of the film counter this reading of *DRT* as an expression of a bleak, postmodern pessimism that would affirm the obsolescence of a modern black politics of the sort typified by Malcolm and Martin. Lee himself later claimed that he is affirming a politics that would embrace aspects of both men, that would use the philosophies and strategies of both for social change in different contexts. He calls attention to the photo put on the wall of the pizzeria as it burns: "Malcolm X and Dr. King are shaking hands and smiling. So when I put those two quotes there, it was not a question of either/or, not for me, anyway, just a choice of tactics. I think they were men who chose different paths trying to reach the same destination against a common opponent."[24]

Thus, on this view, the seemingly opposing quotations of King and Malcolm X that close DRT both articulate valid positions, and which view is more appropriate would depend on the context. Yet the scenario of the film seems to privilege Malcolm X, who would eventually be the topic of Lee's major film epic to date. Indeed, the vision of DRT is in some ways consistent with Malcolm X's black nationalist teachings and thus affirms certain modern political positions. One of the street-corner philosophers expresses wonder and chagrin that a Korean grocer can turn a boarded-up building into a successful business, while Blacks cannot. Surely this is a nod toward Malcolm X's views on black self-sufficiency and economic independence, and certainly Spike Lee has enacted this philosophy as successfully as anyone in the African-American community. Clearly Mookie is going to get nowhere working in Sal's pizzeria and the other homeboys in the movie are also going nowhere. "Time to wake up, brothers, and get your house in order" is an arguable message of the film.

Similarly, Malcolm X placed heavy emphasis on black manhood, standing up to the white power structure, fighting back, and acting decisively to maintain one's self-respect. In that sense, Mookie's violent action exemplifies certain aspects of Malcolm's teachings, though one could question whether this was in fact "the right thing." One could also ask whether Malcolm X did or did not advocate "the right thing" politically at various phases of his life and what his legacy is for us today. I will interrogate X from these perspectives, arguing that the film, like DRT, is ultimately a morality tale and that Lee's politics slide into a black identity politics that can be pinned down neither to specific modern positions (i.e., Martin or Malcolm) nor to postmodern nihilism.

X AS A MORALITY TALE

From my reading of *DRT*, one could argue that *X* is also a morality tale interrogating "the right thing" for Blacks in both the individual and political sense. In this reading, the figure of Malcolm X is the center of the film, and the crucial transitions involve his transformation from criminal to dedicated black nationalist working for the Nation of Islam and subsequently to a more secular internationalist. The key, then, is Malcolm X as moral ideal, as an enlightened model of a black transformation to self-sovereignty.

Although Lee strongly affirms Malcolm X's politics, he is not, I believe, an uncritical sycophant and hagiographer, and brings into question many of Malcolm X's views, while forcing the audience to decide whether the actions of Malcolm or other characters in his films are indeed "the right thing." I thus see *X* and *DRT* as political morality plays and believe that Spike Lee was perfectly justified in telling black and other children to skip school to see the film *X*. In viewing the film, one not only learns a great deal about one of the most important figures of our time, but is forced to reflect upon what is "the right thing" in terms of individual and political morality. I would argue that *X* focuses on Malcolm as a role model for blacks and is more a morality tale than a political drama. Malcolm X certainly exemplifies someone who undergoes profound self-transformation and forges his own identity under difficult circumstances. (The delineation of such righteous models is also congruent with Brechtian strategy.)

The first part of *X*, arguably, shows what the wrong thing is for Blacks today, that is, engaging in a life of crime, drugs, and shallow materialism.[25] Yet Lee invests so much time and energy in this phase of Malcolm's life that the onetime criminal Malcolm Little seems almost attractive and certainly sympathetic.

Though in his autobiography Malcolm X himself presents Malcolm Little as a very bad dude, such an image does not emerge from Lee's film. Denzel Washington creates an engaging character, and Lee's use of comedy and melodrama invests Malcolm Little with appealing qualities. So although he is caught in criminal activity and goes to jail, the film puts a positive spin on his early life, full of high times with white women, drugs, exciting high jinks, and good buddies.[26]

Lee uses the strategy of epic realist historical tableaux in this sequence, heavily seasoned with comedy, satire, and music. As always, music is extremely important in Lee's films. X can be seen and heard as a history of black music and its role in everyday life. Again, there are parallels with Brecht, as Brecht used music to capture the ethos and style of an age and as a way of making, or highlighting, didactic points. Moreover, Lee presents certain forms of black behavior, such as "conking" hair, as bad and the early sequences contain the obvious moral that a life of crime leads to jail. The message concerning black men who involve themselves with white women is not as clear, though Lee tends to present interracial relationships negatively in X and in his other films, such as *Jungle Fever*.[27]

The prison sequence shows Malcolm Little refusing to submit to the humiliations of prison life and then being broken by solitary confinement. But he also comes to accept Black Muslim teachings and betters himself through study. It is one of Lee's pervasive messages that education is the way to "Uplift the Race" (one of the mottoes of *School Daze* and the title of the book on that film), and certainly Malcolm X embodies this philosophy as he learns to study and acquire knowledge. Indeed, Malcolm X emerges from prison a totally changed man and an exemplar of someone who has transformed himself.

As we have seen, X can be read as a Brechtian epic drama or morality tale that conveys lessons for Blacks and others by showing tableaux of social and asocial behavior that contrast positive and negative values. Lee deploys a variety of genres and styles, and mixes music, comedy, and dramatic flashbacks into key episodes of Malcolm X's early life (the mixing of genres is also Brechtian). The last third of the film continues this strategy, though it is too dense and compressed to present adequately Malcolm X's teaching and the complexity of his later positions. The key episode is the shift from Malcolm X's adherence to the teachings of Elijah Muhammad and the Nation of Islam to his radical activist social philosophy. Yet the film presents, arguably, too much of the religious and dubious racial teachings of the Nation of Islam and not enough of Malcolm X's late social philosophy, which many believe is his most valuable radical legacy.[28]

In fact, the film ends, during its title sequence, with the same ambiguity as *DRT,* which alternates images and quotes of Malcolm X and Martin Luther King. *X* concludes with a black gospel song, "Sometime We'll All Be Free," which suggests Christian patience, followed by the song "Revolution" by the radical group Arrested Development. Once again, Lee plays off two opposing political ideologies, but in this film he would seem to privilege a politics of revolution (although, as I have suggested, he also privileges individual change and self-development, taking Malcolm as a role model rather than representative of a specific political philosophy).

In Lee's defense, I should add that he does spend much energy trying to clarify the reasons for Malcolm X's break with the Nation of Islam and portraying Malcolm's transition to a radically new position, again underlying the importance of self-transformation. Lee also deals with the complexity of Malcolm X's assassination and the strong possibility that not just the Nation of Islam but also U.S. government agencies were involved in his murder. Moreover, Lee shows that while he is in Mecca, the "mature" Malcolm sees that all colors are equal. However, I am bracketing the question of historical accuracy in my discussion (to which much of the criticism of the film has been directed, by both Lee's friends and enemies) and am focusing instead on the issue of aesthetic strategy and the politics of the film.[29] In any case, Lee's film on Malcolm X raises the question concerning his own politics, a topic that I take up in the next section.

CULTURE AND POLITICS

In this essay, I have focused on Lee's cultural politics and use of Brechtian aesthetic strategies. Yet there are some major differences between Brecht and Lee. Brecht was a dedicated communist with very specific political values and a fairly specific Marxist political agenda.[30] Lee's politics, by contrast, appear more vague and indeterminate, positioning Lee somewhere between a high modernist stance that refuses any political position, a more pragmatic contextualist politics that draws on disparate sources for specific political interventions in concrete political situations, and an identity politics defined primarily through the production of cultural identity.

On the whole, Lee's cultural politics focus on the specificity of African-American cultural style and identity as the key constituents of a black politics of identity. Such cultural politics are valuable for providing awareness of the distinct forms of oppression suffered by subordinate groups and for making the production of an independent cultural style and identity an important part of the struggle against oppression. But cultural politics might deflect attention and energy from pressing political and economic issues and may well produce a separatist consciousness that undermines a politics of alliance that would mobilize distinct groups against oppressive forces, practices, and institutions.

Hence, I wish to qualify my presentation of Lee as a Brechtian, for I do not think that Malcolm X plays the role that Marx played in Brecht's work, nor, for that matter, does the black radical tradition as a whole play as important a role in Lee's work as the Marxian tradition played in Brecht's work. Lee's politics are, for the most part, culturalist, focusing on black identity and moral decisions concerning race, gender, and personal identity.

This is evident in *DRT,* where Lee interrogates the visible badges of cultural politics and presents the conflicts of the community primarily in cultural terms. Lee excels in presenting small-group dynamics but has not been successful in articulating the larger structures – and structural context of black oppression – that affect communities, social groups, and individual lives. Thus, he does not really articulate the dynamics of class and racial oppression in U.S. society.

This leads to related questions about the representations of gender, race, and class in Spike Lee's films. *DRT* focuses more on gender and race than on class, seeing the antagonism between Italians and Blacks more as a racial conflict than a class conflict. While the small businessman Sal can be seen as a representative of the class system that oppresses Blacks, he, like the Korean grocer, is really part of the ethnic working class himself, even though he owns a small business. Lee claims that he intended to deal with the black working class in *DRT:* "In this script I want to show the black working-class. Contrary to popular belief, we work. No welfare rolls here, pal, just hardworking people trying to make a decent living."[31]

This passage, written before he actually made the film, is curious because the only Blacks shown working are the disc jockey, Mookie, and a black cop. Mookie's sister is said to work, but it isn't clear whether any of the other Blacks are employed. And although the neighborhood is inhabited by what could be called the black underclass, there is no exploration of their oppressive living and working conditions. All of the characters define their identity in terms of fashion, consumption, and cultural style. Only the old drunk, Da Mayor, dresses in a slovenly way, while all of the other characters seem to be full-scale participants in consumer society (much of the film, in fact, concerns the consumption of pizza, ice cream, ice cones, beer, and other drinks, food, and consumer goods, for which everyone always seems to have the money).

Consequently, as I noted earlier, Lee tends to celebrate consumption and to define cultural identity in terms of style and

FIGURE 13
Da Mayor offers Mookie some words of wisdom. (Courtesy of the
Museum of Modern Art, New York.)

consumption patterns. Moreover, he fails to address the reality
and dynamics of class oppression. Reflecting his own middle-
class perspective, most of Lee's characters are middle class and
upwardly mobile Blacks. The protagonists of *She's Gotta Have It*
are middle class, and although some of the students in *School
Daze* represent different classes and status groups, they are at
least upwardly mobile. A scene in a fast-food chicken restaurant
in which the students confront working-class Blacks suggests
hostility between these African-American sectors, but their differences are not adequately explored in Lee's films.[32] *Mo' Better
Blues* and *Jungle Fever* focus on black professionals, and while the
latter has powerful images of a crack house and the degradation
of drug addiction, neither explores black underclass oppression.

Similarly, class and class oppression are not thoroughly examined in *X*. The inner-city Blacks are shown in the beginning of
the film buying zoot suits, getting their hair conked, and dancing in dazzling ballrooms where they can pick up white women.

A scene in which Malcolm is working on a train and fantasizes about pushing food into the face of an obnoxious white male customer depicts race rather than class hatred. In the next scene, Lee shows Malcolm becoming involved in a life of crime when a Harlem crime lord takes him on, suggesting that it is race hatred, rather than class oppression, that pushes Blacks into crime. Nowhere does Lee adequately explore class difference and exploitation. The Malcolm who converts to Islam takes on resolutely middle-class values, and the black underclass almost disappears from the film once he leaves prison and becomes a major political figure.

Thus, Lee projects his own black middle-class values into the characters of all his films. Amiri Baraka claims that Lee "is the quintessential buppie, almost the spirit of the young, upwardly mobile, Black, petit bourgeois professional" and argues that these values permeate his films.[33]

Gender, like race, is a major focus of all of Lee's films, although he has been sharply criticized by black feminists for his treatment of the topic. bell hooks, for example, criticizes Lee's conventional construction of masculinity and stereotypical, usually negative images of women.[34] His male characters often define themselves by acts of violence and typically engage in extreme macho/masculinist behavior. The women are generally more passive and powerless. There are, however, exceptions: Mookie's sister, Jade, and his Puerto Rican wife, Tina, verbally assault the male characters. These examples, however, show Lee's proclivity toward stereotypical images of female "bitchiness," although Jade, played by his sister Joie Lee, is a strongly sympathetic character.

As Michele Wallace notes, Lee privileges conventional heterosexual relationships and stigmatizes oral sex, which, Wallace argues, demeans gays, as well as negatively portraying "the rest of the vast range of illicit sexual practices and psychosocial developments beyond the pale of compulsory heterosexuality, in which such perverse passions as interracial sex and drug addiction are included."[35] In fact, I think that part of the underlying problem with Lee's gender politics is his tendency to use Brecht-ian "typical" characters to depict "typical" scenes. The "typical," however, is a breath away from the stereotypical, archetypal, conventional, representative, average, and so on, and lends itself to caricature and distortion. Lee's characters thus often embody gender or racial stereotypes. He is a "realist" only in Brecht's sense of trying to depict "real" situations, but he does not engage the realities of underclass life or of gender oppression to any great extent. Indeed, like Brecht, he uses comedy, aesthetic inter-ruption, satire, farce, and other devices to confront the problems of race, gender, and sexuality. These are hot issues, and much of the interest in Lee's work resides in his attention to them. Yet one could question whether Lee interrogates gender and sexual-ity any more seriously or successfully than he interrogates class.

There is an almost obsessive focus on skin color in Lee's films. In *School Daze* he divides Blacks according to the color of their skin. In *Jungle Fever* too, there are constant contrasts between light- and dark-skinned Blacks, and the wives of the two main black characters are extremely light-skinned. Both *Fever* and *X* fetishize white women, showing them to be an intense object of black male desire and a route to black male downfall. One of the jazz musician's girlfriends in *Mo' Better Blues* is light-skinned, while the other is dark black. Most of the sex scenes in Lee's films are shot at night and the lighting exaggerates skin color differences.

Yet as others have argued,[36] Lee seems to rule out the possibil-ity of healthy romantic relationships between people of different color – a quasi-segregationist position that a more progressive multiculturalist vision would reject. There are also stereotypical doublings of women between "good" and "bad" in Lee's films, especially evident in *X*, where Malcolm's girlfriend Laura goes from good to bad. Laura is first depicted as Malcolm's good girlfriend, contrasted with the white woman Sophia. Laura, how-ever, becomes a junkie and a whore. Eventually, Malcolm's wife Betty appears as the ultimate good woman, against whom all previous and other women seem "bad." Yet this replicates the

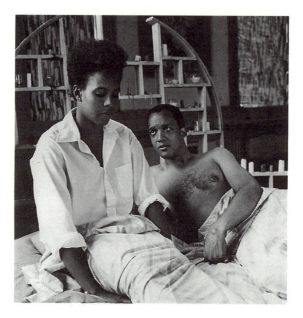

FIGURE 14

Nola Darling (Tracy Camila Johns) and Jamie Overstreet (Redmond Hicks), one of Nola's three lovers in *She's Gotta Have It*. (From the editor's collection.)

stereotypical "Madonna" and "whore" opposition that has dominated a certain type of classical Hollywood cinema. Possible exceptions to these stereotypes in *X* are the Muslim sisters who are seduced and made pregnant by Elijah Muhammad, but they too are ultimately presented as victims, as helpless objects of male desire and as breeding machines to perpetuate a male patriarchy.

Moreover, all of Lee's films relegate women to the sphere of private life, while men are active in public life. This is most striking in *X*, where Malcolm X's wife is depicted primarily as a dutiful spouse, raising his children and standing passively beside him. There are few positive images of women, or of egalitarian relationships between men and women, in Lee's films.[37] Malcolm is shown as a harsh patriarch who seems to want a wife

FIGURE 15

Bleek Gilliam (Denzel Washington) and Clarke Betancourt (Cynda Williams), an aspiring singer and one of Bleek's two girlfriends in *Mo' Better Blues*. (Courtesy of the Museum of Modern Art, New York.)

FIGURE 16

Bleek and Indigo Downes (Joie Lee), a schoolteacher and the girlfriend whom Bleek finally marries in *Mo' Better Blues*. (Courtesy of the Museum of Modern Art, New York.)

primarily for breeding. Flipper in *Jungle Fever* abandons his black wife for a white woman and then this relationship is shown to fail. Nola Darling in *She's Gotta Have It* plays off three black men against each other and the resulting tension harms all her relationships. The jazz musician has two girlfriends in *Mo' Better Blues* and, once again, this situation is shown as untenable; the main character marries the more conventional woman, has a family, and gives up his jazz career.

In part, Lee's sexual politics fall prey to the stereotypes of the classical Hollywood cinema. But they also reflect the male chauvinism in the black and other minority communities and the intensity of conflict between male and female – explosive tensions also articulated in rap music. But his cinema does not explore the causes of these tensions or propose any solutions.

For the most part, Lee privileges morality over politics in his films, which are best viewed as morality tales rather than political learning plays in Brecht's sense.[38] Although his early musical, *School Daze*, thematizes class to some degree, on the whole Lee's films deal more with race and gender than class (which is, of course, a major focus of Brecht's Marxian aesthetic).

Before making my final criticisms, however, I want to stress the progressiveness and excellence of Lee's films in relation to other films produced by major studios. Both aesthetically and politically, his films are far superior to most other Hollywood films. Moreover, Lee is to be commended for his ability to use media culture to articulate African-American perspectives, which are then disseminated through his films and his energetic promotion of them. Yet it is through critique and self-critique that cultural and political progress is made, and Lee has been criticized from within the African-American community for being politically vague and indeterminate and for replacing nitty-gritty issue politics with cultural politics.[39]

Lee tends to reduce politics to cultural identity and slogans. *School Daze* ends with the message "Wake up!" proclaimed by the black activist hero of the movie, and *DRT* begins and ends with the disc jockey Mister Señor Love Daddy admonishing his listeners to do the same. Fine, wake up. But to what, and what does one do when one is awake? Such concrete politics seem beyond the purview of Lee's vision and suggest the limitations of his politics.

Moreover, he seems to be concerned primarily with the situation and oppression of Blacks and not that of other groups. This could be excused on the grounds that someone needs to undertake this effort, yet Lee tends to ignore how a system of exploitation oppresses Blacks and other people of color and oppressed groups. Indeed, Lee's color fetishism aids a divide-and-conquer perspective that, in essence, blinds the colonized and prevents solidarity among the oppressed.[40]

Identity politics helps keep oppressed peoples apart and tends to reduce politics to the search for a cultural identity and style. Lee never portrays political movements in any serious fashion. He fetishizes leaders, which, as Adolph Reed writes,

> also reflects an idea of politics that is antidemocratic and quietistic. Great Leaders don't make movements. Insofar as they aren't just the work of clever publicists, they are in most important respects holograms created by movements. Understanding politics as a story of Great Leaders produces nostalgia and celebration, not mobilization and action.[41]

Although there is a conflict in Lee's work between his affirmation of Malcolm X's modern politics and his evocation of a postmodern political pessimism, it seems to me that the central problem with Lee's politics is that he ultimately comes down on the side of a culturalist identity politics, which subordinates politics in general to the creation of personal identity. Identity for Lee is primarily black identity, and he constantly operates with a binary opposition between black and white, "us" and "them." Lee's identity politics, moreover, are primarily culturalist, in which identity is defined by image and cultural style. This is clearly the case in *DRT*, where every character's politics is defined in terms of cultural style. None of the characters is involved in a political organization, movement, or struggle.

FIGURE 17
Radio Raheem and Buggin' Out as the keepers of the "Dump Koch" wall of fame. Lee's graphic construction displays his political commitment to the mayoral campaign of David Dinkins. Mike Tyson offers a right hook to Mayor Koch, while Jesse Jackson posters demand onlookers to "Get Out and Vote" and remind them that "*Our* Vote Counts!" (From the editor's collection.)

Consequently, Buggin' Out's boycott of Sal's pizzeria is a pathetic caricature of the real struggles by people of color for rights and survival.

Concrete issues of black politics in *DRT* are reduced to graffiti on walls, to slogans like "Tawana Told the Truth," "Dump Koch," or "Jesse," referring to Jesse Jackson's 1988 run for the presidency. As bell hooks notes, Lee never explores alliance politics and fails to realize that

combatting racism and other forms of domination will require that black people develop solidarity with folks unlike ourselves who share similar political commitments. Racism . . . is not erased when we control the production of goods and services in various black communities, or infuse our art with an Afrocentric perspective. Nostalgia for expressions of black style is less and less accessible to black folks who no longer live in predominantly black communities.[42]

Indeed, a genuine emancipatory politics would not limit itself to single-issue or identity politics, but would be open to a politics of otherness, an alliance politics that would identify common interests against oppression. Malcolm came close to this near the end of his life, which is why he was so dangerous. The Nation of Islam doesn't really threaten the white power structure with its segregationist ethos and reverse racism (or with its problematical theology). But a politics of alliance that brings together progressive Blacks, Whites, and other people around an agenda fostering genuine social change and justice could be a powerful force for real social progress.

Lee's politics of identity, by contrast, works primarily to indict racism and to promote the interests of black identity and pride, channeled largely into cultural style. As many critics have argued, Lee ultimately reduces Malcolm X to an image in both *DRT* and *X,* and he uses him to promote the consumption of Malcolm X products. This consumption of Malcolm is superficially expressed as a quest for black identity. Spike Lee thus ultimately falls victim to a consumerist image culture, in which value, worth, and identity are defined in terms of images and cultural style, in which one's image determines who one is and how one will be received.

Film, to be sure, is at its best a feast of images, but critical film interrogates these images, deconstructs those that serve the interests of domination, and develops alternative images, narratives, and aesthetic strategies. Lee, however, does not rise above the repertoire of dominant images already established and reproduces many questionable images of men, women, Blacks, and other races. Although his films show that cinema can address key political issues and generate interesting discussions that may have progressive political effects, so far his films, whatever their merits, are limited, specifically in their identity politics.

Yet Lee's films do attack at least some of the many forms of sex, race, gender, and class oppression. While they might not ultimately provide models of a "counterhegemonic cinema" as bell hooks and other African-American radicals desire, they provide some engaging and provocative cinematic interventions that are far superior to the crass genre spectacles of the Hollywood cinema.

NOTES

This essay was first presented in a syposium on *Malcolm X* organized by Mark Reid for the 1993 Society for Cinema Studies conference and was then presented in a workshop on contemporary film at the American Sociology Association. Special thanks to Steve Best, Harvey Cormier, Cynthia Freeland, Rhonda Hammer, Kelly Oliver, Mark Reid, and Thomas Wartenberg for comments on earlier versions.

1. There has been much debate concerning what terminology to use in describing black people of African-American descent in the United States. Following what seems to be the current convention, I use the term "Blacks" and "African-Americans" interchangeably, though some prefer "Afro-American" and some prefer to leave out the hyphen. To me the hyphen usefully signifies the cultural duality and tensions in the experiences of Blacks in the Americas who have both an African origin and American roots and experience.

2. Ed Guerrero, *Framing Blackness: The African American Image in Film* (Philadelphia: Temple University Press, 1993), p. 113.

3. In *Framing Blackness,* Guerrero also claims that in times of a general slump, Hollywood invests in low-budget black films to raise the profit margin, whereas it ignores African-American films when profits are high and the industry has "no need to continue a specifically black-focused product line" (p. 165).

4. Alex Patterson, *Spike Lee: A Biography* (London: Abacas, 1992), pp. 55, 92, 121. Patterson notes that Lee's *She's Gotta Have It* cost only $175,000 and pulled in over $8.5 million; *School Daze* was budgeted at $5.8 million and took in more than $15 million; *Do the Right Thing* was budgeted at $6.5 million and grossed over $25 million. Many of Lee's films have also been profitable in the video-cassette

market. Evidently, the money made on these films persuaded the Hollywood money establishment that Lee and other young black directors were marketable and funded a burgeoning black cinema in the early 1990s; also see Guerrero, *Framing Blackness,* p. 157, and Patterson, *Spike Lee,* p. 223. In *Redefining Black Film* (Berkeley: University of California Press, 1993), however, Mark A. Reid notes that Lee's films draw on earlier black cinema: "Lee's film journals never recognize his debt to other black filmmakers, yet he borrows from their cinematic portrayals of urban black life and their use of contemporary black music" (p. 107).

5. I am aware that there are problems with a white male professional in a privileged race, class, and gender position writing about African-American culture and politics, but I would argue that it is important for people of different identities to explore the terrain of difference and otherness. I consulted with a number of African-American and feminist critics on this project and am grateful to many people for their comments.

6. I do not know whether Brecht specifically influenced Lee, or if Lee (re)invented something like a Brechtian cinema from his own experiences and resources. I have not yet found any references to Brecht in the book publications that Lee regularly produces on his films, and have found only one mention of a possible Brecht–Lee connection in the growing literature on the black director. Paul Gilroy, in a critique of Lee in the *Washington Post* (November 17, 1991), notes that like those of "Brecht, who has influenced him so much," Lee's "loudly declared political commitments only end up trivializing the political reality at stake in his work and thereby diminishing its constructive political effect." But other than this (contestable) statement, Gilroy and other critics have not yet explored Lee's appropriation of Brecht's aesthetic strategies. For a fuller presentation of Brecht's aesthetics and politics see Douglas Kellner, "Brecht's Marxist Aesthetic: The Korsh Connection," in *Bertolt Brecht: Political Theory and Literary Practice,* Betty Weber and Herbert Heinin, eds. (Athens: University of Georgia Press, 1981), pp. 29–42.

7. See Roland Barthes, *The Pleasure of the Text* (New York: Oxford University Press, 1975), on "the writerly" modernist text that requires an active reader.

8. Fredric Jameson, in *Signatures of the Visible* (New York: Routledge, 1990) and *Postmodernism, or the Cultural Logic of Late Capitalism* (Durham, NC: Duke University Press, 1991), stresses the role of individual vision and style in modernism, while Peter Burger, in *Theory of the*

Avant-Garde (Minneapolis: University of Minnesota Press, 1974, repr. 1984), analyzes the "historical avant-garde" that attempts to change art and life, as opposed to more formalistically oriented modernist art.

9. This reading was suggested in conversation by Zygmunt Bauman after a series on postmodern film at the Summer 1992 10th Anniversary Conference, "Theory, Culture, & Society." In addition, Lee's *DRT* is read as a "postmodern" film in a somewhat indeterminate sense in Norman Denzin, *Images of Postmodern Society* (Newbury Park, CA: Sage Press, 1991), p. 125. Likewise, in "Spike Lee and the Commerce of Culture," in *Black Cinema*, Manthia Diawara, ed. (New York: Routledge, 1993), Houston A. Baker describes Lee in *DRT* as a "true postmodern" with an "astute, witty, brilliant critique of postmodern, urban hybridity," but without giving the term "postmodern" any substance. I will argue later that Lee basically grounds his politics and aesthetic strategies in modernist positions and is not in any important sense "postmodernist." (Baker's article is a reprint of an article of the same title in *Black American Literature Forum* 25:1 [Summer 1991]: 237–52.)

10. Of course, there are many postmodern politics, ranging from the nihilism of the post-1980s Jean Baudrillard to the pragmatic reformism of Jean-François Lyotard and Richard Rorty to the multiculturalist identity politics of many women and minority group postmoderns; see the survey in Steven Best and Douglas Kellner, *Postmodern Theory* (New York: Macmillan and Guiford Press, 1991).

11. Denzin, *Images of Postmodern Society*, p. 125.

12. Here, Lee pays homage to the Robert Mitchum character in *Night of the Hunter*, who was, however, quite evil; thus, Lee's appropriation of this symbolism perhaps inadvertently codes Raheem as more negative than Lee intended. In Spike Lee with Lisa Jones, *Do the Right Thing: A Spike Lee Joint* (Simon & Schuster, 1989), Lee writes, "I want to pay homage to *Night of the Hunter*. You know those brass knuckle name rings that kids are wearing now? They're gold-plated and spread across four fingers. Radio Raheem will wear two of these. The one on his left hand will read 'L-O-V-E,' on his right, 'H-A-T-E,' just like Robert Mitchum's tattoos. . . . Radio Raheem tells Mookie a story about the rings that will be a variation on Robert Mitchum's tale of his tattoos. Vicious" (p. 78).

13. Lee indicates that he disapproves of African-American youth exhibiting gold chains and the like ("They don't understand how worthless that shit is in the long run"), but doesn't criticize this form of

consumerism in the film and in fact reinforces it in his cinematic images and capitalist ventures. For Lee's disclaimers, see *Do the Right Thing*, pp. 59 and 110.

14. Patterson, *Spike Lee*, p. 125.

15. Ibid. Here Patterson notes some criticisms of Lee's commercial activity.

16. bell hooks, *Yearning, Race, Gender and Cultural Politics* (Boston: South End Press, 1990), p. 179. hooks complains that a stuttering, inarticulate black youth is chosen to represent the profoundly intelligent and articulate views of Malcolm X and Martin Luther King.

17. See Benedict Anderson, *Imagined Communities* (New York: Verso Press, 1983).

18. Put differently, Lee's portrayal of racism does not take into account logical types – the fact that there is a hierarchy of racial virulence that is usually dictated by color (Blacks being subject to the most extreme racism, followed by Hispanics, Asians, and ethnics like Italians). Other hierarchies are those of gender (with women below men), sexual preference (with gays the object of heterosexuals' prejudice) and so on, such that black, lesbian women suffer significantly more oppression than, say, Hispanic men. The scene under question, however, portrays all forms of racism in terms of linguistic equivalence of cultural difference and racial hatred. (I am grateful to Rhonda Hammer for this insight.)

19. As Guerrero puts it in *Framing Blackness*: "By constructing Buggin' Out and Radio Raheem as supercilious and unreasonable characters, advocating the most effective social action instrument of the civil rights movement, the economic boycott, and then having the possibility of social action dismissed by the neighborhood youth for the temporary pleasures of a good slice of pizza, the film trivializes any understanding of contemporary black political struggle, as well as the recent history of social movements in this country. This dismissal of collective action is further accented by contrasting Buggin' Out and Raheem with the character of Mookie, the film's calculating middle-man, positioned between Sal and the community. For it is through Mookie's aloof, individualist perspective that much of the film is rendered" (p. 149).

20. In interviews after the release of the film, Lee said that he was constantly amazed that people were indignant over the destruction of property, but that few of these people focused on the black youth's death. Lee was initially concerned to interrogate the conditions that could lead to the wanton killing of black youth, spurred

on by the Howard Beach killings in which white youths gratu-
itously assaulted some black youths, leading to one of their deaths.
Thus, Lee seems to believe that violent protest is a legitimate response to the senseless killing of Blacks, as would, presumably,
Malcolm X.

In his book *Do the Right Thing,* Lee remarks: "The character I play
in *Do the Right Thing* is from the Malcolm X school of thought: 'An
eye for an eye.' Fuck the turn-the-other-cheek shit. If we keep up
that madness we'll be dead. YO, IT'S AN EYE FOR AN EYE" (Lee's
capitals; p. 34).

21. This reading was suggested by Kelly Oliver in a comment on an
    earlier draft of my essay. Indeed, as indicated in note 20, Lee was
    angry because many viewers and reviewers seemed very upset by
    the destruction of property, but overlooked the fact that a black
    youth was killed by the police.

22. In a throwaway line, Mookie's sister, Jade, mentions that she'd like
    to see something positive happen for the community, but it isn't
    clear what she has in mind and in the absence of a more complete
    development of her political views, one can only guess.

23. It is precisely this nihilism that Cornel West warns Blacks against
    in "Nihilism in Black America," in *Black Popular Culture,* Gina Dent,
    ed. (Seattle: Bay Press, 1992), pp. 37–47.

24. Spike Lee with Ralph Wiley, *By Any Means Necessary: The Trials and
    Tribulations of the Making of "Malcolm X"* (New York: Hyperion,
    1992), p. 5.

25. The reviews of *Jungle Fever* generally overlooked the fact that a good
    part of the film was spent attacking the crack scene, portraying it as
    a dead end and a major force of destruction in the black commu-
    nity. Lee avoided the issue of drugs, however, in his earlier films,
    for which he was criticized.

26. Brecht too was sympathetic to criminals and often presented them
    favorably, as in the *Three-Penny Opera.* At times, they were op-
    pressed proletarians, though Brecht also used gangster figures to
    represent capitalists and fascists.

27. Although the narrative suggests that Malcolm was attracted to the
    white woman Sophia as a means of exerting sexual power and
    gaining racial revenge, the relationship is more favorably presented
    than the interracial relationships in *Jungle Fever,* despite the fact
    that Malcolm X came to sharply condemn black men's pursuit of
    white women. I discuss Lee's controversial sexual politics later in
    this essay.

28. The Nation of Islam, for instance, preached black superiority, pre-

sented the white man as a "devil," and in general engaged in racist teachings, advocating black separatism rather than structural social transformation. For some years, Malcolm X shared this perspective, but eventually distanced himself from it and developed more revolutionary and internationalist perspectives. See collections of Malcolm X's later writings such as *The Final Speeches* (New York: Pathfinder Press, 1992).

29. Obviously, the question of historical accuracy is important in evaluating a film that makes the pretense of telling the truth about Malcolm X's life. Lee's book on the making of the film indicates that he was attempting to uncover the truth of Malcolm's life through research and interviews, so one could legitimately examine the film for its historical accuracy; such a project, however, goes beyond the scope of this essay. For some reflections on the historical correctness and distortions of *X*, see the symposium in *Cineaste* 19:4 (1993): 5–18 and the review by bell hooks, "Malcolm X: Consumed by Images," *Z Magazine* (March 1993): 36–39.

30. There is some debate about this. See Kellner, "Brecht's Marxist Aesthetic," pp. 29–42.

31. Lee with Jones, *Do the Right Thing*, p. 30.

32. See Reid, *Redefining Black Film*, pp. 98–100. Reid discusses this scene and its dramatization of class schisms within the African-American community.

33. Amiri Baraka, "Spike Lee at the Movies," in *Black Cinema*, p. 146.

34. hooks, *Yearning*, p. 173.

35. Michele Wallace, "Boyz N the Hood and Jungle Fever," in *Black Popular Culture*, p. 129.

36. hooks, *Yearning*; Wallace, "*Boyz N the Hood* and *Jungle Fever*"; Guerrero, *Framing Blackness*; and Mark A. Reid, "The Brand X and Post-Negritude Frontier," *Film Criticism* 20:1–2 (Fall–Winter 1995–96): 17–25.

37. A curious set of images for interpreting Lee's sexual politics are found in the opening dance by Rosie Perez in *Do the Right Thing*. In *Yearning*, hooks notes how this dance replicates male behavior (male dance forms, boxing, fighting, etc.). But Lee possibly intends it to be a powerful image of a woman of color, since the dance is accompanied by the rap song "Fight the Power." It is a striking but ambiguous sequence, perhaps signaling the film's modernism, which requires viewers to construct their own readings.

38. For Brecht, a political learning play would impart exemplary political insights and behavior to its audience, helping to politicize them and incite them to participate in social change. It is not clear

whether Lee's films function in this way or, as I am arguing, serve instead as black morality tales.

39. For two interesting discussions of this problem, see Adolph Reed, "The Trouble with X," *Progressive* (February 1993): 18–19, and Baraka, "Spike Lee at the Movies," p. 145.
40. Cornel West, "A Matter of Life and Death," *October* 61 (Summer 1992): 20–27.
41. Reed, "The Trouble with X," p. 19.
42. hooks, *Yearning,* pp. 183–84. Also see the discussion of these issues in bell hooks and Cornel West, *Breaking Bread* (Toronto: Between the Lines, 1992).

5 The Violence of Public Art

DO THE RIGHT THING

In May 1989 I tried unsuccessfully to attend an advance screening of Spike Lee's *Do the Right Thing* (*DRT*) at the University of Chicago. Students from the university and the neighborhood had lined up for six hours to get the free tickets, and none of them seemed interested in scalping them at any price. Spike Lee made an appearance at the film's conclusion and stayed until well after midnight answering the questions of the overflow crowd. This event turned out to be a preview not simply of the film, but of the film's subsequent reception. Lee spent much of the summer answering questions about the film in television and newspaper interviews; the *New York Times* staged an instant symposium of experts on ethnicity and urban violence; and screenings of the film (especially in urban theaters) took on the character of festivals, with audiences in New York, London, Chicago, and Los Angeles shouting out their approval to the screen and to each other.

The film elicited disapproval from critics and viewers as well. It was denounced as an incitement to violence and even as an *act* of violence by viewers who regarded its representations of ghetto characters as demeaning.[1] The film moved from the familiar commercial public sphere of "culture consumption" into the sphere of public art, the arena of the "culture-debating" public, a shift signaled most dramatically by its exclusion from the "Best Picture" category of the Academy Awards. As the film's early reception subsides into the cultural history of the late 1980s in the United States, we may now be in a position to assess its significance as something more than a "public sensation" or "popular phenomenon." *DRT* is rapidly establishing itself not only as a work of public art (a "monumental achievement" in the trade lingo), but as a film *about* public art.[2] The film tells a story of multiple ethnic public spheres, the violence that circulates among and within these partial publics, and the tendency of this violence to fixate on specific images – symbolic objects, fetishes, and public icons or idols.

The specific public image at the center of the violence in *DRT* is a collection of photographs, an array of signed publicity photos of Italian-American stars in sports, movies, and popular music framed and hung on the "Wall of Fame" in Sal's Famous Pizzeria at the corner of Stuyvesant and Lexington Avenues in Brooklyn. A young bespectacled man named "Buggin' Out" (who is the closest thing to a "political activist" to be found in this film) challenges this arrangement, asking Sal why no pictures of black Americans are on the wall. Sal's response is an appeal to the rights of private property: "You want brothers up on the Wall of Fame, you open up your own business, then you can do what you wanna do. My pizzeria, American-Italians only up on the wall." When Buggin' Out persists, arguing that Blacks should have some say about the wall since their money keeps the pizzeria in business, Sal reaches for a baseball bat, a publicly recognizable emblem of both the American way of life and recent white-on-black violence. Mookie, Sal's black delivery boy (played by Spike Lee), defuses the situation by hustling Buggin' Out from inside the pizzeria. In retaliation, Buggin' Out tries, quite unsuccessfully, to organize a neighborhood boycott, and the conflict between the black public and the private white-owned business simmers on the back burner throughout the hot summer day. Smiley, a stammering, semiarticulate black man

FIGURE 18
Mookie and Sal with the "Wall of Fame" in the background above the heads of Sal's black patrons. (Courtesy of the Museum of Modern Art, New York.)

who sells copies of a unique photograph showing Martin Luther King and Malcolm X together, tries to sell his photos to Sal (who seems ready to be accommodating) but is driven off by Sal's son Pino. Sal is assaulted by another form of "public art" when Radio Raheem enters the pizzeria with his boom box blasting out Public Enemy's rap song "Fight the Power." Finally, at clos-ing time, Radio Raheem and Buggin' Out reenter Sal's, radio blasting, to demand once again that some black people go up on the Wall of Fame. Sal smashes the radio with his baseball bat; then Raheem pulls Sal over the counter and begins to choke him. In the riot that follows, the police kill Radio Raheem and depart with his body, leaving Sal and his sons to face a neighbor-hood uprising. Mookie throws a garbage can through the win-dow of the pizzeria, and the mob loots and burns it. As the fire

Distinction between public space and private ownership.

smolders, Smiley enters the ruins and pins his photograph of King and Malcolm to the Wall of Fame.

Sal's Wall of Fame exemplifies the central contradictions of public art. It is located in a place that may be described, with equal force, as a public accommodation and a private business. Like the classic liberal public sphere, it rests on a foundation of private property, which comes into the open when its public inclusiveness is challenged. Sal's repeated refrain throughout the film to express both his openness and hospitality to the public and his "right" to reign as a despot in his "own place" is a simple definition of what his "place" is: "This is America." As "art," Sal's wall stands on the threshold between the aesthetic and the rhetorical, functioning simultaneously as ornament and as propaganda, both a private collection and a public statement. The content of the statement occupies a similar threshold, which is the hyphenated space designated by "Italian-American," a hybrid of particular ethnic identification and general public identity. The wall is important to Sal not just because it displays famous Italians but because they are famous *Americans* (Frank Sinatra, John Travolta, Joe DiMaggio, Sylvester Stallone, Liza Minnelli, Mario Cuomo) who have made it possible for Italians to think of themselves as Americans, full-fledged members of the general public sphere. The wall is important to Buggin' Out because it signifies exclusion from the public sphere. This may seem odd, since the neighborhood is filled with public representations of African-American heroes on every side: a huge billboard of Mike Tyson looms over Sal's pizzeria; children's art ornaments the sidewalks and graffiti streaks subversive messages like "Tawana Told the Truth" on the walls; Magic Johnson T-shirts, Air Jordan sneakers, and a variety of jewelry and exotic hairdos make the characters like walking billboards for "black pride." The sound-world of the film is suffused with a musical "Wall of Fame," a veritable anthology of great jazz, blues, and popular music emanating from Mister Señor Love Daddy's storefront radio station, just two doors away from Sal's (see Chapter 3 by Victoria Johnson).

Why aren't these tokens of black self-respect enough for Bug-gin' Out? The answer, I think, is that they are only tokens of self-respect, of black pride, and what Buggin' Out wants is the respect of Whites, the acknowledgment that African-Americans are hy-phenated Americans too, just like Italians.[3] The public spaces accessible to Blacks in the film are *only* public, and only in the special way that the sphere of commercial-industrial publicity (a sphere that includes, of course, movies themselves) is available to Blacks. They are, like the public spaces in which black athletes and entertainers appear, rarely owned by Blacks themselves; they are reminders that black public figures are largely the "property" of a white-owned corporation – whether a professional sports franchise, a recording company, or a film distributor. The public spaces in which Blacks achieve prominence are thus only sites of publicity or of marginalized arts of resistance, the disfiguring of public spaces epitomized by graffiti, not of a genuine public sphere they may enter as equal citizens. The spaces of publicity, despite their glamour and magnitude, are not as important as the humble little piece of "real America" that is Sal's pizzeria, the semiprivate, semipublic white-owned space, the threshold space that supports genuine membership in the American public sphere. The one piece of public art "proper" that appears in the film is an allegorical mural across the street from Sal's, and it is conspicuously marginalized; the camera never lingers on it long enough to allow decipherment of its complex images. The mural is a kind of archaic residue of a past moment in the black struggle for equality, when "black pride" was enough. In *DRT* the Blacks have plenty of pride; what they want, and cannot get, is the acknowledgment and respect of Whites.

The film does not suggest, however, that integrating the Wall of Fame would solve the problem of racism or allow African-Americans to enter the public sphere as full-fledged Americans. Probably the most fundamental contradiction the film suggests about the whole issue of public art is its simultaneous triviality and monumentality. The Wall of Fame is, in a precise sense, the "cause" of the major violence in the narrative, and yet it is also

FIGURE 19

Left: Ossie Davis stars as Da Mayor, a philosophical drunkard. *Right:* Ruby Dee stars as Mother Sister, a wise matron. (From the editor's collection.)

merely a token or symptom. Buggin' Out's boycott fails to draw any support from the neighborhood, which generally regards his plan as a meaningless gesture. The racial integration of the public symbol, as of the public accommodation, is merely a token of public acceptance. Real participation in the public sphere involves more than tokenism: it involves full economic participation. As long as Blacks do not own private property in this society, they remain in something like the status of public art, mere ornaments to (or disfigurations of) the public place, entertaining statues and abstract caricatures rather than full human beings.

Spike Lee has been accused by some critics of racism for projecting a world of black stereotypes in his film: Tina, the tough, foul-mouthed sexy ghetto babe; Radio Raheem, the sullen menace with his ghetto blaster; "Da Mayor," the neighborhood wino;

"Mother Sister," the domineering, disapproving matriarch who sits in her window all day posed like Whistler's mother. Lee even casts himself as a type, a streetwise, lazy, treacherous hustler who hoards his money, neglects his child, and betrays his employer by setting off the mob to destroy the pizzeria. But it is not enough to call these stereotypes "unrealistic." They are, from another point of view, highly realistic representations of the public *images* of blacks: the caricatures imposed on them and (sometimes) acted out by them. Ruby Dee and Ossie Davis, whom Lee cast as the Matriarch and the Wino, have a long history of participation in the film proliferation of these images, and Dee's comment on the role of black elders is quite self-conscious about this history: "When you get old in this country, you become a statue, a monument. And what happens to statues? Birds shit on them. There's got to be more to life for an elder than that."[4] The film suggests that there should be more to life for the younger generation as well, which seems equally in danger of settling into a new image-repertoire of stereotypes. It is as if the film wanted to cast its characters as publicity images with human beings imprisoned inside them, struggling to break out of their shells to truly participate in the public space where they are displayed.

This "breaking out" of the public image is what the film dramatizes and what constitutes the violence that pervades it. Much of this violence is merely trivial or irritating, involving the tokens of public display, as when an Irish yuppie homesteader (complete with Larry Bird T-shirt) steps on Buggin' Out's Air Jordans; some is erotic, as in Tina's dance as a female boxer, which opens the film; some is subtle and poetic, as in the scene when Radio Raheem breaks out of his sullen silence, turns off his blaster, and does a rap directly addressed to the camera, punctuating his lines with punches, his fists clad in massive gold rings that are inscribed with the words "Love" and "Hate." Negative reactions to the film tend to focus obsessively on the destruction of the pizzeria, as if the violence against property were the only "real" violence in the film. Radio Raheem's murder

FIGURE 20
Mookie shares a tender moment with Tina, the mother of his son.
(From the editor's collection.)

is regularly passed over as a mere link in the narrative chain that leads to the climactic spectacle of the burning pizzeria. Spike Lee has also been criticized for showing this spectacle at all; the film has routinely been denounced as an incitement to violence or at least a defense of rioting against white property as an act of justifiable violence in the black community. Commentators have complained that the riot is insufficiently motivated, or that it is just there for the spectacle, or to prove a thesis.[5] In particular, Spike Lee has been criticized for allowing Mookie's character to "break out" of its passive, evasive, uncommitted stance at the crucial moment, when he throws the garbage can through the window.

Mookie dramatizes the whole issue of violence and public art by staging an act of vandalism against a public symbol and specifically by smashing the plate glass window that marks the boundary between public and private property, the street and

the commercial interest. Most of the negative commentary on
the film has construed this action as a political statement, a call
by Spike Lee to advance African-American interests by trashing
white-owned businesses. Lee risks this misinterpretation, of
course, in the very act of staging this spectacle for potential
monumentalization as a public statement, a clearly legible image
readable by all potential publics as a threat or model for imita-
tion. That this event has emerged as the focus of principal controversy suggests that it is not so legible, not so transparent as it
might have seemed. Spike Lee's motives as writer and director –
whether to make a political statement, give the audience the
spectacle it wants, or fulfill a narrative design – are far from clear.
And Mookie's motivation as a character is equally problematic:

FIGURE 21

Jade and her brother, Mookie, slightly blocking the graffiti "Tawana
Told the Truth." Mookie warns Jade to avoid Sal and his Italian
sausage. (From the editor's collection.)

at the very least, his action seems subject to multiple private determinations – anger at Sal, frustration at his dead-end job, rage at Radio Raheem's murder – that have no political or "public" content. At the most intimate level, Mookie's act hints at the anxieties about sexual violence that we have seen encoded in other public monuments. Sal has, in Mookie's view, attempted to seduce his sister, Jade (whom we have seen in a nearly incestuous relation to Mookie in the opening scene), and Mookie has warned her never to enter the pizzeria again. (This dialogue is staged in front of the pizzeria's brick wall, spray-painted with the graffiti message "Tawana Told the Truth," an evocation of another indecipherable case of highly publicized sexual violence.) Mookie's private anxieties about his manhood ("Be a man, Mookie!" is his girlfriend Tina's hectoring refrain) are deeply inscribed in his public act of violence against the public symbol of white domination.

But private, psychological explanations far from exhaust the meaning of Mookie's act. An equally compelling account would regard the smashing of the window as an ethical intervention. At the moment of Mookie's decision the mob is wavering between attacking the pizzeria and assaulting its Italian-American owners. Mookie's act directs the violence away from persons and toward property, the only choice available in that moment. One could say that Mookie does "the right thing," saving human lives by sacrificing property.[6] Most fundamentally, however, we have to say that Spike Lee himself does "the right thing" in this moment by breaking the illusion of cinematic realism and intervening as the director of his own work of public art, taking personal responsibility for the decision to portray and perform a public act of violence against private property. This choice breaks the film loose from the *narrative* justification of violence, its legitimation by a law of cause and effect or political justice, and displays it as a pure effect of *this* work of art in this moment and place. The act makes perfect sense as a piece of Brechtian theater, giving the audience what it wants with one hand and taking it back with the other.

We may call *DRT* a piece of "violent public art," then, in all the relevant senses – as a representation, an act, and a weapon of violence. But it is a work of *intelligent* violence, to echo the words of Malcolm X that conclude the film. It does not repudiate the alternative of nonviolence articulated by Martin Luther King in the film's other epigraph (this is, after all, a film, a symbolic and not a "real" act of violence); it resituates both violence and nonviolence as strategies within a struggle that is simply an ineradicable fact of American public life. The film may be suffused with violence, but unlike the "Black Rambo" films that find such ready acceptance by the American public, *DRT* takes the trouble to differentiate this violence with ethically and aesthetically precise images. The film exerts a violence on its viewers, badgering us to "fight the power" and "do the right thing," but it never underestimates the difficulty of rightly locating the power to be fought or the right strategy for fighting it. A prefabricated propaganda image of political or ethical correctness, a public monument to "legitimate violence" is exactly what the film refuses to be. It is, rather, a monument of resistance, of "intelligent violence," a ready-made assemblage of images that reconfigures a local space – literally, the space of the black ghetto, figuratively, the space of public images of race in the American public sphere. Like the Goddess of Democracy in Tiananmen Square, which I will discuss later, the film confronts the disfigured public image of legitimate power, holding out the torch of liberty with two hands, one inscribed with "Hate," the other with "Love."

COMMERCIAL FILM AND PUBLIC ART

The juxtaposition of commercial film and public art illuminates a number of contrasting features whose distinctiveness is under considerable pressure, both in recent film practice and in contemporary art. An obvious difference between the movies and public art is the contrast in mobility. The movies "move" in every possible way – in their presentation, their circulation and distribution, and their responsiveness to the fluctuations of contemporary taste. Of all forms of art and in contrast to the movies, public art is the most static, stable, and fixed in space: the monument is a fixed, generally rigid object, designed to remain on its site for all time.[7] Public art is supposed to occupy a pacified, utopian space, a site held in common by free and equal citizens whose debates, freed of commercial motives, private interest, or violent coercion, will form "public opinion." Movies are viewed in private, commercial theaters that further privatize spectators by isolating and immobilizing them in darkness. Public art stands still and silent while its beholders move in the reciprocal social relations of festivals, mass meetings, parades, and rendezvous. Movies appropriate all motion and sound to themselves, allowing only the furtive, private rendezvous of lovers or of autoeroticism.

The most dramatic contrast between film and public art emerges in the characteristic tendencies of each medium with respect to the representation of sex and violence. Public art tends to repress violence, veiling it with the stasis of monumentalized and pacified spaces, just as it veils gender inequality by representing the masculine public sphere with the monumentalized bodies of women. Film tends to express violence, staging it as a climactic spectacle, just as it foregrounds gender inequality by fetishizing rather than monumentalizing the female body. Sex and violence are strictly forbidden in the public site, and thus the plaza, common, or city square is the favored site for insurrection and symbolic transgression, with disfiguration of the monument a familiar, almost ritual occurrence.[8] The representation of sex and violence is licensed in the cinema, and it is generally presumed (even by the censors) that it is reenacted elsewhere – in streets, alleys, and private places.

I have rehearsed these traditional distinctions between film and public art not to claim their irresistible truth but to sketch the conventional background against which the relations of certain contemporary practices in film and public art may be understood – their common horizon of resistance, as it were. Much recent public art obviously resists and criticizes its own site, and the fixed, monumental status conventionally required of it; much of it aspires, quite literally, to the condition of film in the form of photographic or cinematic documentation. I have discussed how a particular film creates forms of resistance and mirrors the economy of violence encoded in public images. I now will discuss how a similar political and artistic impulse to social inequity inspired an "unauthorized" creation of a public art.[9]

BUGGIN' OUT MEETS THE GODDESS OF TIANANMEN SQUARE

In May 1988, I took what may well be the last photograph of the statue of Mao Tse Tung on the campus of Beijing University. The thirty-foot monolith was enveloped in a bamboo scaffolding "to keep off the harsh desert winds," my hosts told me with knowing smiles. That night, workers with sledgehammers reduced the statue to a pile of rubble, and rumors spread throughout Beijing that the same thing was happening to Mao statues on university campuses all over China. One year later, most of the world's newspaper readers scanned the photos of Chinese students erecting a thirty-foot styrofoam and plaster "Goddess of Democracy" directly facing the disfigured portrait of Mao in Tiananmen Square despite the warnings from government loudspeakers: "This statue is illegal. It is not approved by the government. Even in the United States statues need permission before they can be put up."[10] A few days later the newspaper accounts told us of army tanks mowing down this statue along with thousands of protesters, reasserting the rule of what was called "law" over a public and its art.

The Beijing massacre, and the confrontation of images at the central public space in China, is full of instruction for anyone who wants to think about public art and, more generally, of the whole relation of images, violence, and the public sphere.[11] "Even in the United States" political and legal control is exerted, not only over the erection of public statues and monuments, but over the display of a wide range of images, artistic or otherwise, to actual or potential publics. Even in the United States, the "publicness" of public images goes well beyond their specific sites or sponsorship: "publicity" has, in a very real sense, made all art into public art. And even in the United States, art that enters the public sphere is liable to be received as a provocation to or an act of violence.

This juxtaposition of the politics of American public art with the monumental atrocities of Tiananmen Square has struck some readers as deeply inappropriate. Zhang Longxi has argued that it is a "rather casual use of the Chinese example," one that "seems to trivialize the momentum of a great and tragic event" and "verges on endorsing the Chinese government's view" while failing to understand the "true meaning of that phrase" – "even in the United States" – "coming out of government loudspeakers."[12] My aim, of course, is not to endorse the Chinese government's massacre of its people, but to see what might be learned from its manner of legitimating that massacre. The government's verbal pretensions of legality and public civility coupled with the most transparent visual representations of brutal violence effectively dismembered and disarticulated the smooth suturing of the television news image-text. But the spectacle does more than undermine the phrase, revealing it as a cynical alibi for state repression. It also puts the phrase into a new orbit of global circulation and connects it, albeit anachronistically and a-topically, with other public spectacles of monumental violence and violence against monuments. "Even in the U.S." comes home to roost, as it were, and the question is how. This sort of juxtaposition and circulation is what it means to live in a society of spectacle and surveillance, the world of the pictorial turn. Zhang Longxi is right to worry that such specular linkages risk trivializing great and tragic events. But the ability to differentiate and connect the trivial and the tragic, the insignificant and the monumental, is precisely what is at issue in the critique of art, violence, and the public sphere. Above all, the relations of literal and figurative violence, of violence by and against persons, and violence by and against images can be measured only at the risk of trivializing the monumental and vice versa.

Our own historical moment in the United States has seemed especially rich in examples of public acts and provocations that cross the boundaries between real and symbolic violence, between the monumental and trivial. The erosion of the boundary between public and private spheres in a mediatized, specular society is what makes those border crossings possible, even inevitable. Recent art has carried the scandals previously associated with the cloistered spaces of the art world – the gallery, the museum, and the private collection – into the public sphere. And the public, by virtue of governmental patronage of the arts, has taken an interest in what is done with its money, no matter whether it is spent on traditional public art – in a public place as a public commission – or on a private activity in a private space that just happens to receive some public support or publicity. The controversy over Richard Serra's "Tilted Arc" sculpture in a public plaza in New York City marks one boundary of this phenomenon. Serra's is a traditional work of public art; it provoked another engagement in what Michael North has called the "tiresome battle, repeated in city after city . . . whenever a piece of modern sculpture is installed outdoors."[13] But now the battle has moved indoors, into the spaces of museums and art schools. The privacy of the exhibition site is no longer a protection for art that does symbolic violence to revered public figures like the deceased mayor of Chicago or to public emblems and icons like the American flag or the crucifix.

The erosion of the boundary between public and private art is accompanied by a collapsing of the distinction between symbolic and actual violence, whether the "official" violence of police, juridical, or legislative power or the "unofficial" violence in the responses of private individuals. Serra's "Tilted Arc" was seen as a violation of public space, was subjected to actual defacement and vandalism by some members of the public, and became the subject of public legal proceedings to determine whether it should be dismantled.[14] The official removal of an art student's caricature of Mayor Washington from the School of the Chicago Art Institute involved not just the damaging of the offensive picture, but a claim that the picture was itself an "incitement to violence" in black communities. A later installation at the same school asking "What Is the Proper Way to Display the American Flag?" was construed as an invitation to "trample" on the flag. It immediately attracted threats of unofficial violence against the person of the artist and may ultimately serve as the catalyst not simply for legislative action but for a constitutional amendment protecting the flag against all acts of symbolic or real violence. The response to Andres Serrano's "Piss Christ" and the closing of the Mapplethorpe show at the Corcoran Gallery indicate the presence of an American public, or at least of some well-entrenched political interests, that is fed up with tolerating symbolic violence against religious and sexual taboos under the covers of "art," "privacy," and "free speech" and is determined to fight back with the very real power of financial sanctions.[15] The United States is nowhere near to sending tanks to mow down students and their statues, but it has recently endured a period when art and various partial publics (insofar as they are embodied by state power and "public opinion") have seemed on a collision course.

THE VIOLENCE OF PUBLIC ART

We may now be in a position to measure the gap between the tragic events of the spring of 1989 in China and the impact of a Hollywood film that just happened to be released at the same moment. The gap between the two events, and the images that brought them into focus for mass audiences, may seem too great for measurement. But it is precisely the distance between the monumental and the trivial, between violence in the "other country" and our own, that needs to be assessed if we are to construct a picture, much less a theory, of the circulation of visual culture in our time. The Goddess of Democracy imaged a short-lived utopian and revolutionary monument that seems to grow in stature as it recedes in memory. It brought briefly into focus the possible emergence of a democratic, civil society in a culture and political order that has endured the violence of state repression for centuries. DRT deploys its utopian, revolutionary rhetoric on a much smaller stage (a street in Brooklyn), and its challenge to established power is much more problematic and equivocal. If the Goddess claimed to symbolize the aspirations of a majority, an all-inclusive public sphere, then Spike Lee's film articulates the desperation of a minority, a partial public, calling on the majority to open the doors to the public sphere promised by its official rhetoric. The violence in DRT may be local, symbolic, even "fictional" in contrast to the Tiananmen Square massacre, but it refers unequivocally to the widespread, unrelenting, and very real violence against African-Americans in the United States, both the direct physical violence of police repression instantiated by Radio Raheem's murder and the long-term economic violence perpetrated by the white majority.

Perhaps the most obvious contrast between the Goddess and DRT is the sense (doubtless inaccurate)[16] that the former is an image of revolutionary "purity," the latter a highly impure image-repertoire of compromises, trade-offs, and sellouts. The harshest criticism that has been made of Spike Lee is the claim that he is merely another "corporate populist," franchising his own celebrity as a star and director, trading in his progressive principles for advertising contracts with the Nike Corporation.[17] The advantage of this ad hominem attack is that it saves a lot of time: one needn't actually look at DRT (or at Spike Lee's witty, ironic commercials for Nike), because one already knows that he is a capitalist.

On the other hand, if one is willing to grant that corporate capital constitutes the actual, existing conditions for making movies with any chance of public circulation, then one actually has to look at the work and assess its value.[18] *DRT* makes abundant sense as a film *about* corporate populism, a critique of the effects of capital in a multiethnic American community. The film shows what it is like to live in a community where no utopian public image or monument is available to symbolize collective aspirations, a community where personal identity is largely constituted by commodity fetishism – from Air Jordan sneakers to Magic Johnson jerseys to designer jewelry and elephantine boom boxes.

The meaning of these fetishes, however, is not confused with the labeling of them as fetishistic. They are treated critically, with irony, but without the generalized contempt and condescension generally afforded to "mere" fetishes. Radio Raheem's blaster is as important to him as Sal's pizzeria (and the Wall of Fame) is to him. Both are commercial objects *and* vehicles for the propagation of public statements about personal identity. Even the image in the film that comes closest to being a sacred, public totem, the photograph of King and Malcolm X shaking hands, has been turned by Smiley into a commodity. The affixing of this image, with all of its connotations of love and hate, violence and nonviolence, to the smoldering remains of the Wall of Fame is the closest the film comes to the sort of apotheosis achieved by the Goddess of Democracy as she faced the disfigured portrait of Mao.

If *DRT* has a moral for those who wish to continue the tradition of public art and public sculpture as a utopian venture, a "daring to dream" of a more humane and comprehensive public sphere, it is probably in the opening lines of the film, uttered by the ubiquitous voice of Love Daddy: "Wake up!" Public art has always dared to dream, projecting fantasies of a monolithic, uniform, pacified public sphere, a realm beyond capitalism and outside history. What seems called for now, and what many contemporary artists wish to provide, is a *critical* public art that is frank about the contradictions and violence encoded in its own situation, one that dares to awaken a public sphere of resistance, struggle, and dialogue. Exactly how to negotiate the border between struggle and dialogue, between the argument of force and the force of argument, is an open question, as open as the two hands of the Goddess of Democracy or the two faces of revolution in Smiley's photograph.

NOTES

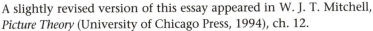

A slightly revised version of this essay appeared in W. J. T. Mitchell, *Picture Theory* (University of Chicago Press, 1994), ch. 12.

1. Murray Kempton's review (*New York Review of Books* [September 28, 1989], pp. 37–38) is perhaps the most hysterically abusive of the hostile reviews. Kempton condemns Spike Lee as a "hack" who is ignorant of African-American history and guilty of "a low opinion of his own people" (p. 37). His judgment of Mookie, the character played by Spike Lee in the film, is even more vitriolic: Mookie "is not just an inferior specimen of a great race but beneath the decent minimum for humankind itself" (p. 37).

2. One of the interesting developments in the later reception of *DRT* has been its rapid canonization as Spike Lee's "masterpiece." Critics who trashed the film in 1989 now use it as an example of his best, most authentic work in order to trash his later films (most notably *Malcolm X*).

3. I am indebted to Joel Snyder for suggesting this distinction between self-respect and acknowledgment.

4. Quoted in Spike Lee with Lisa Jones, *Do the Right Thing: A Spike Lee Joint* (Simon & Schuster, 1989), p. 79, caption to plate 30.

5. Terrence Rafferty ("Open and Shut," review of *Do the Right Thing*, *New Yorker*, July 24, 1989) makes all three complaints. Rafferty (1) reduces the film to a thesis about "the inevitability of race conflict in America"; (2) suggests that the violent ending comes only from "Lee's sense, as a filmmaker, that he needs a conflagration at the end"; and (3) compares Lee's film unfavorably with Martin Scorsese's *Mean Streets* and *Taxi Driver*, where "the final bursts of violence are generated entirely from within." What Rafferty fails to consider is (1) that the film explicitly articulates theses that are diametrically opposed to his reductive reading (most notably, Love Daddy's concluding call, "My people, my people," for peace and harmony, a speech

filled with echoes of Zora Neale Hurston's autobiography); (2) that the final conflagration might be deliberately staged – as is so much of the film – *as a stagey, theatrical event* to foreground a certain requirement of the medium; (3) that the psychological conventions of Italian-American neorealism with their "inner" motivations for violence are among the issues under examination in *DRT*.

6. This interpretation was first suggested to me by Arnold Davidson, who heard it from David Welberry of the Philosophy Department at Stanford University. It received independent confirmation from audiences of this essay at Harvard, California Institute of the Arts, Williams College, University of Southern California, University of California, Los Angeles, Pasadena Art Center, the University of Chicago's American Studies Workshop, the Chicago Art History Colloquium, and Sculpture Chicago's conference "Art in Public Places." I wish to thank the participants in these discussions for their many provocative questions and suggestions.

7. The removal of "Tilted Arc" is all the more remarkable (and ominous) in view of this strong presumption in favor of permanence.

8. The fate of the Berlin Wall is a perfect illustration of this process of disfiguration as a transformation of a public monument into a host of private fetishes. While the Wall stood it served as a work of public art, both in its official status and in its unofficial function as a blank slate for the expression of public resistance. As it is torn to pieces, its fragments are carried away to serve as trophies in private collections. As German reunification proceeds, these fragments may come to signify a nostalgia for the monument that expressed and enforced its division.

9. By the phrase "economy of violence," I mean, quite strictly, a social structure in which violence circulates and is exchanged as a currency of social interaction. The "trading" of insults might be called the barter or "in-kind" exchange; body parts (eyes, teeth notably) can also be exchanged, along with blows, glares, hard looks, threats, and first strikes. This economy lends itself to rapid, runaway inflation, so that (under the right circumstances) an injury that would have been trivial (stepping on someone's sneakers, smashing a radio) is drastically overestimated in importance. As a currency, violence is notoriously and appropriately unstable.

10. Uli Schmetzer, *Chicago Tribune* (June 1, 1989): 1.

11. For an excellent discussion of the way the events in China in June 1989 became a "spectacle for the West," overdetermined by the presence of a massive publicity apparatus, see Rey Chow, "Violence in the Other Country: Preliminary Remarks on the 'China Crisis,'

June 1989," *Radical America* 22 (July–August 1989): 23–32. See also Wu Hung, "Tiananmen Square: A Political History of Monuments," *Representations* 35 (Summer 1991): 84–117.

12. Zhang Longxi, "Western Theory and Chinese Reality," *Critical Inquiry* 19:1 (Autumn 1992): 114.

13. Michael North, *The Final Sculpture: Public Monuments and Modern Poets* (Ithaca, NY: Cornell University Press, 1985), p. 17. "Tilted Arc" is "traditional" in its legal status as a commission by a public, governmental agency. In other ways (style, form, relation to site, public legibility) it is obviously nontraditional.

14. For an excellent account of this whole controversy and the decision to remove "Tilted Arc," see Sherrill Jordan et al., eds., *Public Art/ Public Controversy: The Tilted Arc on Trial* (New York: American Council for the Arts, 1987).

15. On the neoconservative reactions against controversial forms of state-supported art in the late 1980s, see Paul Mattick, Jr., "Arts and the State," *Nation* 251:10 (1 October 1990): 348–58.

16. The "purity" of the Goddess of Democracy is surely compromised by the mixture of sources and motives that went into its production and effect. As Wu Hung notes, "it was not a copy" of the Statue of Liberty, and yet it "owed its form and concept" to "other existing monuments" – most notably the image of "a healthy young woman," specifically "a female student" – to stand for a new concept of the public sphere ("Tiananmen Square," p. 110). The students' motives, moreover, ranged from revolutionary idealism to "mere" reform of government corruption and the hope for opportunities in more open exchanges with capitalist economies. Some observers, no doubt, saw the statue as an appeal to the true spirit of Maoism beneath the disfigured portrait.

17. This charge is made by Jerome Christensen in "Spike Lee, Corporate Populist," *Critical Inquiry* 17:3 (Spring 1991): 582–95. A more detailed rejoinder is provided in my "Seeing *Do the Right Thing*," in the same issue, pp. 596–608.

18. One of the more astonishing claims of Christensen's essay is that Lee's filmmaking is "the most advanced expression of the emergent genre of corporate art" (p. 589), a development in which "films . . . are rapidly being transformed into moving billboards for corporate advertising" (p. 590). This "emergence" and "transformation" will be news to film historians who have traced the links between corporate advertising and filmmaking to the earliest days of the industry. See Miriam Hansen on the commodification of the teddy bear in early cinema in her "Adventures of Goldilocks: Spectatorship,

Consumerism, and Public Life," *Camera Obscura* 22 (January 1990): 51–71, and Jane Gaines, *Contested Culture: The Image, the Voice, and the Law* (Chapel Hill: University of North Carolina Press, 1991), especially her analysis of commodity "tie-ups" – "the consumer goods and services that have been linked with the release of motion pictures" (p. xiii).

Filmography

STUDENT FILMS AT NEW YORK UNIVERSITY

1980

The Answer
Director: Spike Lee
Screenplay: Spike Lee
Editing: Spike Lee

1981

Sarah
Director: Spike Lee
Screenplay: Spike Lee
Editing: Spike Lee

1982

Joe's Bed-Stuy Barbershop: We Cut Heads
Director: Spike Lee
Screenplay: Spike Lee
Editing: Spike Lee

FEATURE FILMS

1986

She's Gotta Have It
Director: Spike Lee
Screenplay: Spike Lee
Cinematographer: Ernest Dickerson
Editing: Spike Lee
Production company/distributor: Forty Acres and a Mule Filmworks /
   Island Pictures
Cast: Tracy Camila Johns, Redmond Hicks, John Canada Terrell, Spike
   Lee, Raye Dowell

1988

School Daze
Director: Spike Lee
Screenplay: Spike Lee
Cinematographer: Ernest Dickerson
Editing: Barry Alexander Brown
Production company/distributor: Forty Acres and a Mule Filmworks /
   Columbia Pictures
Cast: Lawrence Fishburne, Giancarlo Esposito, Spike Lee, Tisha Cam-
   bell, Kyme, Joie Lee, Joe Seneca, Art Evans, Ellen Holly, Ossie Davis

1989

Do The Right Thing
Director: Spike Lee
Screenplay: Spike Lee
Cinematographer: Ernest Dickerson
Editing: Barry Alexander Brown
Production company/distributor: Forty Acres and a Mule Filmworks /
   Universal Pictures
Cast: Danny Aiello, Ossie Davis, Ruby Dee, Richard Edson, Giancarlo Es-
   posito, Spike Lee, Bill Nunn, John Turturro, Paul Benjamin, Frankie
   Faison, Robin Harris, Joie Lee, John Savage

Making "Do The Right Thing"
Director: St. Clair Bourne
Cinematographers: Juan Lobo, Joseph Friedman

Editing: Susan Fanshel
Production company/distributor: Chamba Productions and Forty Acres
and a Mule Filmworks / First Run Features
Cast: Spike Lee

1990

Mo' Better Blues
Director: Spike Lee
Screenplay: Spike Lee
Cinematographer: Ernest Dickerson
Editing: Sam Pollard
Production company/distributor: Forty Acres and a Mule Filmworks /
Universal Pictures
Cast: Denzel Washington, Spike Lee, Wesley Snipes, Giancarlo Esposito, Robin Harris, Joie Lee, Bill Nunn, John Turturro, Dick Anthony
Williams, Cynda Williams

1991

Jungle Fever
Director: Spike Lee
Screenplay: Spike Lee
Cinematographer: Ernest Dickerson
Editing: Sam Pollard
Production company/distributor: Forty Acres and a Mule Filmworks /
Universal Pictures
Cast: Wesley Snipes, Annabella Sciorra, Spike Lee, Ossie Davis, Ruby
Dee, Samuel L. Jackson, Lonette McKee, John Turturro, Frank Vincent, Anthony Quinn

1992

Malcolm X
Director: Spike Lee
Screenplay/adaptation: Arnold Perl and Spike Lee; from Alex Haley's *The Autobiography of Malcolm X*
Cinematographer: Ernest Dickerson
Editing: Barry Alexander Brown
Production company/distributor: Forty Acres and a Mule Filmworks /
Warner Brothers

Cast: Denzel Washington, Angela Bassett, Albert Hall, Al Freeman, Jr.,
Delroy Lindo, Spike Lee

1994

Crooklyn
Director: Spike Lee
Screenplay: Joie Susanah Lee, Cinque Lee, Spike Lee
Cinematographer: Arthur Jafa
Editing: Barry Alexander Brown
Production company/distributor: Forty Acres and a Mule Filmworks /
Universal Pictures
Cast: Alfre Woodard, Delroy Lindo, Spike Lee, Zelda Harris

1995

Clockers
Director: Spike Lee
Screenplay/adaptation: Richard Price and Spike Lee; from a Richard Price
novel of the same title
Cinematographer: Malik Hassan Sayeed
Editing: Sam Pollard
Production company/distributor: Forty Acres and a Mule Filmworks /
Universal Pictures
Cast: Harvey Keitel, John Turturro, Delroy Lindo, Mekhi Phifer, and
Isaiah Washington

1996

Get on the Bus
Director: Spike Lee
Screenplay: Reggie Rock Bythewood
Cinematographer: Elliot Davis
Editing: Leander T. Sale
Production company/distributor: Forty Acres and a Mule Filmworks /
Columbia Pictures
Cast: Charles Dutton, Ossie Davis, André Braugher, DeAundre Bonds,
Wendell Pierce, Isaiah Washington, Roger Guenveur Smith, Thomas
Jefferson Byrd, Albert Hall, Richard Belzer, Joie Lee

Girl 6

Director: Spike Lee
Screenplay: Suzan-Lori Parks
Cinematographer: Malik Hassan Sayeed
Editing: Sam Pollard
Production company/distributor: Forty Acres and a Mule Filmworks / Fox Searchlight
Cast: Theresa Randle, Spike Lee, Isaiah Washington, Debi Mazar, Ron Silver, John Turturro, Jenifer Lewis, Quentin Tarantino, Madonna, Naomi Campbell

ADDITIONAL FILMS CITED

Boyz N the Hood, dir. John Singleton (Columbia, USA, 1991)
Cry Freedom, dir. Richard Attenborough (Universal, USA, 1987)
Friday, dir. F. Gary Gray (New Line Cinema, USA, 1995)
Glory, dir. Edward Zwick (Tri-Star Pictures, USA, 1990)
Godfather, The, dir. Francis Ford Coppola (Paramount, USA, 1972)
Hard Day's Night, A, dir. Richard Lester (GB, 1964)
Help!, dir. Richard Lester (GB, 1965)
House Party, dir. Reginald Hudlin (New Line Cinema, USA, 1990)
Juice, dir. Ernest Dickerson (Paramount, USA, 1992)
Kuhle Wampe, dir. Slaton Dudow (Germany, 1932)
Last Temptation of Christ, The, dir. Martin Scorsese (Universal, USA, 1988)
Mean Streets, dir. Martin Scorsese (Taplin–Perry–Scorsese, USA, 1973)
Menace II Society, dir. Allen and Albert Hughes (New Line Cinema, USA, 1993)
Mr. Deeds Goes to Town, dir. Frank Capra (Columbia, USA, 1936)
Mr. Smith Goes to Washington, dir. Frank Capra (Columbia, USA, 1939)
New Jack City, dir. Mario Van Peebles (Warner Bros., USA, 1991)
Night of the Hunter, The, dir. Charles Laughton (United Artists, USA, 1955)
Rocky, dir. John Avildsen (United Artists, USA, 1976)
Super Fly, dir. Gordon Parks, Jr. (Warner Bros., USA, 1972)
Sweet Sweetback's Baadasssss Song, dir. Melvin Van Peebles (Cinemation, USA, 1971)
Taxi Driver, dir. Martin Scorsese (Columbia, USA, 1976)

Reviews of *Do the Right Thing,* 1989–1990

SPIKE LEE SPOTLIGHTS RACE RELATIONS

JAY CARR

Picture a boiling day in Brooklyn. Picture an escalation of tempers between the white owner of a pizzeria and a couple of his black customers, ending with a black man killed by a white cop and the pizzeria being torched. It's too bloodless to call *Do the Right Thing,* Spike Lee's new film opening Friday at the Nickelodeon, the anatomy of a riot. But part of what gives the film its urgency is its sense of impending explosiveness. Depending on where you're coming from, *Do the Right Thing* is either an unflinching and cautionary look at race relations or an incitement to riot.

"I don't think that's gonna happen," says Lee, looking laid-back yet wary in a Boston hotel suite as he fields the incitement-to-riot question. "It's not a preaching film. The title is ambiguous. Everyone in the film is acting according to their version of the right thing. But I do feel that what the cops do is not the right thing. I don't know what it will take to improve race relations. I think anyone expecting Spike Lee to give answers to that is going to be disappointed. My job is to put the spotlight on race relations in this country. Hopefully, it will provoke thought and discussion. Hopefully, we can move in the direction of ending all this madness. I just think right now the state of race relations in America, and especially in New York, isn't that good."

Lee, 32, lives in Brooklyn and attributes the problems in New York to Mayor Edward L. Koch's last 12 years in office. "He's the mayor," says Lee. "The city follows the mayor, just as the country follows the president. This country has leaned to the right under Reagan. Given his court appointments, his legacy is going to be with us long afterward. The leaders set a tone. The message that's been going out in New York is, 'Keep those niggers in line.' " "Originally, the Howard Beach incident gave me inspiration," Lee continues, referring to the 1986 incident in Queens in which whites attacked and chased three blacks from a pizzeria, causing one to die when he ran into traffic.

The film is dedicated to Michael Griffith, the Howard Beach victim. "I didn't want to do a dramatization of Howard Beach, although I kept a few of the elements – the pizza parlor, the death of a black male, the baseball bat. I knew at the end I wanted the black folks to take a stand." There's an understanding between Sal, the pizzeria owner, and Mookie, the delivery man Lee plays, at the end, Lee explains, "but I didn't want to strike a false note with that. It's a very shaky truce. None of this everybody join hands and sing 'We Are the World.' I just don't think that's realistic at this time in America."

"One of the biggest lies going is that no matter what race, creed or religion you are, it doesn't matter, we're all Americans. That's a lie. Always has been. Just ask the Native American Indians. I want people to feel the horror at the end of the movie. I want people to know that if we don't talk about the problems and deal with them head on, they're going to get much worse. Sure, the heat is an important element in the story, but it's dangerous to put too much emphasis on that. Howard Beach happened in the middle of December – a cold December."

The film's Bedford-Stuyvesant setting is the real thing. Lee, who grew up in Brooklyn, knows it first hand. His NYU graduation film, *Joe's Bed-Stuy Barbershop: We Cut Heads,* was made there. That's the difference between Lee and such black superstars as Eddie Murphy,

Oprah Winfrey and Michael Jackson. Although Lee is the college-educated son of college-educated parents (his father is the composer and musician, Bill Lee), his films clearly speak for black urban Americans who remain virtually invisible in American film.

"Just because Eddie Murphy is the No. 1 movie star and Prince and Michael Jackson are the No. 1 music stars, and Michael Jordan is the No. 1 basketball star, that doesn't mean everything is OK," Lee says. "There's a huge black underclass, and what they face on a daily basis is what my movie is about. Sure, Sal loses his pizzeria, but insurance will replace it. The chief sufferers are the residents in that block." Lee adds that he doesn't see any contradiction between the quotes from Martin Luther King and Malcolm X with which he ends the film, the first advocating nonviolence, the second advocating violence in self-defense. "I really see the lives of Martin Luther King and Malcolm X as intertwined," Lee says. "To me, the thing was where they wanted to end up, not the different routes they chose to get there. They both wanted a world that was humane and just."

The making of the film, in ironic contrast to its subject matter, was smooth, Lee says. "It really just flowed. I wrote it in two weeks. We had to build the pizzeria, the radio station and the Korean grocery store sets on empty lots. The pizzeria looked so real that people kept coming in for slices. As a goodwill gesture, to let the people there know we needed their cooperation, we had a block party. They were very interested in technical things. They wanted to know the procedures – roll, cut, action. We were able to use some of them in the crowd scenes. We couldn't use more because of Screen Actors Guild restrictions."

Lee dismisses questions about the absence of drugs in the film. "I thought racism was enough of a subject for one film," he says. "Actually, we closed three crack houses. We used the Fruit of Islam" – a Black Muslim cadre – "for security, and they closed them down. They're still closed. I just went back there last Saturday." What about the green Larry Bird T-shirt worn by a not particularly enlightened white character in the film? Is Lee sending some message? Lee, a well-known basketball fan, laughs. "No, I just like to get my little jibes in at Larry," he says in the tone of a New York fan who has watched Bird chew up the Knicks. "It's a movie, and there is humor in it."

Nor was there any backwash from the fact that his real-life sister, Joie Lee, plays his sister in the film. "We didn't have any complications at all. Once the film begins, we treat it like a business proposition. I don't let things slide. If anything, I'm harder on my relatives." The fact that Lee grew up around music doesn't mean his next film, "Love Supreme," about a musician played by Denzel Washington, is autobiographical. "It's more fictional than anything else," Lee says. "It's about how a trumpet player tries to balance his music and his love life. Unlike *Round Midnight* or *Bird,* it's contemporary, and reflects the fact that it's harder to make a living playing jazz today. How's jazz going to compete against Michael Jackson and Prince?

"Beyond that, I have no idea. With me, it's always just the next film. With *Do the Right Thing,* I had full artistic control. I made the film I wanted to make." This contrasted with Lee's last film, *School Daze,* over which executives for a different studio nervously hovered. Lee's films have been moneymakers. *She's Gotta Have It* cost $175,000 and grossed $8 million. *School Daze* cost $6.2 million and grossed $18 million. The *Do the Right Thing* budget was $6.5 million. Will he stay in that range? Lee shakes his head nooooo. "These films have been relatively cheap. I gotta move from that low-rent district," he says. Maybe to a more optimistic view of race relations? "Long-term, I'm more optimistic than pessimistic," Lee says. "Whatever happens, that day's going to come. It's not going to happen overnight, though, and no film's going to change things overnight."

BOSTONIANS REVIEW *DO THE RIGHT THING*

PAMELA REYNOLDS

Do the Right Thing, according to Spike Lee, was inspired by the Howard Beach racial incident of 1986, in which a gang of whites attacked three black men and chased them from a Queens pizzeria. The movie, set in a poor black neighborhood in Bedford-Stuyvesant on the hottest day of the year, is a complex work that attempts to explore a number of issues, from police brutality to teen-age pregnancy, to issues of parental responsibility, to the racism pervasive among all ethnic groups, to what means blacks should take toward economic and social empowerment.

As the film opens, it looks as if things will proceed along peaceably enough. Sal, a white pizzeria owner, opens his business, firing up his pizza ovens as he has done for more than 20 years and asking his employee Mookie, played by Spike Lee, to begin his work as a delivery boy. The neighborhood shows the usual signs of life: people gossiping, teen-agers strutting, kids frolicking around a hydrant, the Korean grocer across the street opening his fruit stand. A character by the name of Radio Raheem parades up and down the street carrying his monstrous boom box. Mookie finds the time to visit his girlfriend and their child, whom he visits only every couple of weeks. Every so often, the police come nosing down the street in cruisers.

It is not until late in the day that trouble starts. It begins when two characters, Buggin' Out and Radio Raheem, confront Sal, the pizzeria owner, over the fact that he has no pictures of blacks among the photos of famous Italians in his restaurant. Buggin' Out demands that he put someone black on the wall. Sal refuses. Tempers flare. Tensions escalate. A fight breaks out, with the resulting melee pushing out onto the street. Finally, the cops arrive, handcuffing Buggin' Out and applying a choke-hold to Radio Raheem. The crowd of blacks witnessing the incident converges into an angry mob as they remember past incidents of police brutality in New York.

Mookie, distraught and frustrated by what has just happened, throws a trash can through the window of Sal's pizzeria and a riot ensues, with the angry mob torching the business that had served the neighborhood for more than two decades. The movie ends on a contradictory note in which Lee juxtaposes two conflicting quotes. One quote, spoken by Martin Luther King, excoriates violence as senseless and destructive. The other, spoken by Malcolm X, justifies violence as intelligent and understandable when it is committed in self-defense. Spike Lee challenges the audience to choose.

The movie has received criticism nationally from those who say the story line and characters are stereotypes of blacks and that Lee copped out by not including drugs in his movie. Some have also criticized the filmmaker for not having the guts to take a position on the issues he raised. Still others say the movie is just plain dangerous, given race relations in this country at this time.

Felicia Harden, 19, of Mattapan, however, begs to differ, at least on one point. It couldn't have been more realistic.

"It really impacted on me because it was just like the stuff that happens every day, all the time, in Boston," said Harden, a college student at Wellesley majoring in black studies and Chinese. "I just related it to the gang stuff that's happening . . . the Humboldt gang and the Intervale gang, 'coming on my turf,' stuff like that. It was very realistic. So realistic that it depressed me."

Even the most negative images of blacks, which some middle-class blacks might deride as stereotypical, are real, according to those who have seen the film. Richmond says the Bedford-Stuyvesant block depicted in the film reminded him of an area of Dorchester where the roller skating rink Chez Vous is located. There is a pizzeria owned by some Syrians across the street similar to the one in the movie, a Chinese restaurant in the area like the Korean fruit stand in the movie, and certainly, he says, plenty of kids on the bus with boom boxes.

Alvin Poussaint, associate professor of psychiatry at Harvard Medical School who saw the film at a private screening last week, agrees that the characters Lee presented have some basis in fact.

"A lot of people are going to think the characters are stereotypes, but it would be hard for me to say that blacks don't recognize some of themselves in those characters," he says. "I grew up in East Harlem and I felt it had a lot of reality to it. I saw the people I had known, the men sitting on the corner, the men walking around in anger. It caught a lot of the tone, a lot of the flavor of the inner city . . . the antagonism, the cussing, the not being sure where to go with your life."

Still, Georgopulos feels there were stereotypes that might overwhelm the more subtle complexities of character Lee attempted to bring out in the movie.

"There is a danger of reductionism," she says.

While some, like Poussaint, praise the movie for its honest exploration of issues, others feel there may be something to fears that the film may spark violence. Lee, they say, should have given his audience greater guidance in exploring the issue of violence.

Tischa Brown, exiting the movie, wondered if people would "take it the wrong way."

Felicia Harden says that she could feel palpable tension in the air leaving the theater.

"That's what we're worried about, if people are going to get the message," she says. "People just don't understand the movie. It's sort of defeating the purpose for some of these people to go. They're going to come out of the movie hyped up."

"I felt that people could do violence after seeing this movie," agrees Richmond.

Lee, himself, has responded to such fears by saying that it is not his job to preach an answer to the audience. The film, he says, was meant to force the audience to choose their own answers.

"My job is to put the spotlight on race relations," he said in a recent interview.

If that was Lee's intent, many would agree that he has been successful.

"It's going to raise a lot of discussion between blacks and whites and among blacks themselves," says Poussaint. "People sat in the theater afterwards because they were so affected. It shows things in their complexity."

"I think it's the role of the artist to elevate our consciousness of the conflict," says Georgopulos. "I give him credit for doing a magnificent job."

SPIKE LEE'S WARNING ABOUT RACE RELATIONS IN AMERICA

CLARENCE PAGE

When Spike Lee appeared at a recent preview of his new movie *Do the Right Thing* on the University of Chicago campus, a black woman in the audience thanked him for "having the courage to show us as we really are."

Indeed he does. In *Do the Right Thing,* the perceptive young filmmaker who gave us a sexy and hilarious portrait of black singles in *She's Gotta Have It* and a provocative view of black campus life in *School Daze*, offers a powerful comedy-turned-tragedy about relations between blacks and other races in a modern urban setting and, with that, a powerful warning about where race relations in this country may be heading.

This is a slice of modern urban life too hot for most filmmakers to handle. It is the real New York City of Bernhard Goetz, Howard Beach, Al Sharpton, and "wilding." But it could just as easily be Chicago or any other city where a large socially and politically isolated minority lives in uneasy and resentful coexistence with other groups who seem, even in the era of civil rights reforms and Bill Cosby, to be doing better than blacks.

We meet Sal (played by Danny Aiello), an Italian-American who drives into the neighborhood every day to sell slices at his pizzeria with his two sons, easy-going Vito (Richard Edson) and stone-cold racist Pino (John Turturro).

We meet Mookie (Spike Lee), who delivers pizzas for Sal and spars rhetorically with Pino about subjects ranging from Michael Jordan to Louis Farrakhan.

We meet Radio Raheem (Bill Nunn), a hulking misunderstood home-boy who constantly blasts "Fight the Power" by Public Enemy, the angriest trio in rap music, out of his enormous boom box; and Buggin' Out (Giancarlo Esposito), a loudmouth militant who, like Radio Raheem, frays everyone's nerves.

A family of Koreans run a grocery across the street from Sal's Famous Pizzeria. A trio of aging black men hug a nearby corner and provide running commentary like a Greek chorus. A pair of white cops, about as welcome in this neighborhood as an army of occupation, cruise ominously.

Change the location and you could find these elements of street life in the inner-city ghettoes of just about any major American city, from Chicago to Newark to Atlanta to Los Angeles. Put them all together on the hottest day of the year and you know something is going to blow. On Spike Lee's street, it blows up when the death of a black youth in police hands sparks an ugly race riot in which a crowd of blacks burns down what to them is a major symbol of white power.

Powerful stuff. Some might even call it dangerous. At least one critic has called the film an open invitation to violence. But if you think this movie is going to put you in for a couple hours of raving polemics, you would be wrong. It is a thoroughly entertaining film in a chilling way.

Lee fleshes out his characters well. Lee is more fair to whites in this movie than most filmmakers, caught up in the convenience of easy stereotypes, are to blacks. There are no clear-cut "good guys" or "bad guys" here. Lee shows admirable balance as he explores the ambivalent, contradictory feelings whites have about blacks, feelings that can run from warm love to cold contempt and, perhaps most dangerous, benign indifference.

Sal, for example, properly admonishes his son, Pino, for his blatantly racist attitudes and defends the good neighbors who have kept him in business over the years. Yet Sal draws the line with his own symbol of ethnic pride, his pizzeria's "Wall of Fame" on which prominent celebrities who have Italian roots are displayed.

When Buggin' Out demands to know why a pizzeria with an exclusively black clientele has no "brothers" like Martin Luther King or Malcolm X on its walls, Sal advises him sternly to open his own pizzeria and display whomever he pleases.

Good advice, the late Malcolm might say, but to the aimless and angry Buggin' Out, it is just one more grinding irritation.

Similarly, the trio of black men who hug the nearby corner gripe about how Koreans and other immigrants can come to this country penniless, yet own and operate their own business within a couple of years while the surrounding community sinks deeper into poverty.

With the perceptive eye that has made Lee a treasure among black filmmakers, he deftly portrays the complex, ambivalent, sometimes contradictory ways we African Americans view ourselves, the direct result of what W. E. B. DuBois called the "double consciousness" that comes from being African and American, a condition that churns constant internal debate over how far we can venture into the mainstream of a white-dominated society without losing ourselves.

When Lee was asked at the University of Chicago showing whether he thought the film's riot was justified, he noted how a number of critics, all of them white, also had asked about the "property damage" at the end of the film, but none showed similar concern for whether police were justified in taking the black life lost in the controversial police action that sparked the riot. A pervasive double standard that dismisses black life as less important than white-owned property lies at the heart of this nation's racial troubles, Lee observed.

It also appears to lie at the heart of *Do the Right Thing.* Lee dedicates his film to the families of Eleanor Bumpers, Michael Griffith, Arthur Miller, Edmund Perry, Yvonne Smallwood and Michael Stewart, black New Yorkers killed by police in highly controversial incidents.

In the end, I thought it was a brilliant film, the best anatomy of black anger in a comedy motif I have seen since *Watermelon Man,* a late 1960's film in which the late black actor Godfrey Cambridge plays a white executive who mysteriously turns black one night, finds out that skin color makes a dramatic difference in his middle-class life and, in the end, becomes angry enough to join a "self-defense" class conducted by militant black nationalists.

It also is a deeply disturbing film because it argues so well for a doomsday view of race relations, unless we see a dramatic change in course that does not appear to be on the horizon.

What is the direction black anger should take? Lee appears to offer us a choice by way of two quotes at the end of his film. One from Martin Luther King, Jr., the prince of nonviolence, speaks of the fruitless and self-destructive nature of violence in pursuit of justice. The other from Malcolm X opposes violence for the sake of violence, but eloquently justifies violence for the sake of "self-defense."

Both quotes received enthusiastic applause from the mostly young and racially mixed audience at the University of Chicago, but from different hands. Lee said afterwards that he leans toward the Malcolm quote. King's nonviolent approach would be devoured in today's cynical world, he said.

Lee has said in interviews that he wanted to avoid a sentimental ending that says we are all the same under our skin because it simply would not be true. He's right. Too much time and cultural divergence divide the masses of American blacks and whites. A jolly Hollywood-style ending would not, as a young lady at U. of C. said, show us – black, white, etc. – as we really are.

If anything, *Do the Right Thing* invites us, as divided racial groups, to get reacquainted with each other and ourselves. He also, in his clever way, leaves important questions on our minds:

If immigrants like the Korean family can succeed with inner-city capitalism, why not blacks? If white businesses like Sal's can prosper with black dollars, why not show blacks a little more respect? If the mayor can call a blue-ribbon investigating commission into session to investigate inner-city tensions after a riot, why not during peace?

Spike Lee may ruffle feathers with this film but he also provides a tremendous public service. With his candid account of interracial issues our liberal society is too often too timid to face, he offers a powerful [story] about the course we are taking as a society, unless we do the right thing.

Lee does not try to provide all the answers, but he has a brilliant way of raising the questions.

THIS PICTURE'S AS GOOD AS *THE GODFATHER*

GENE SISKEL

What will Italians think of Spike Lee's new movie? Two friends of mine operate a small Chicago-area restaurant much like Sal's Famous Pizzeria in *Do the Right Thing,* a film in which white cops strangle a young black man after he and a buddy demand that photos of famous blacks be included on Sal's Italian-American Wall of Fame. A race riot ensues and Sal's restaurant is torched.

We saw the film at a preview, and during the screening the two restaurant-owning brothers laughed at everything from the fulsome arguments among the Italian family to the way one black customer mispronounced mozzarella as "moose-a-rella." But the screening room went quiet after the black youth was killed and Sal's restaurant was destroyed.

Here's what the brothers had to say immediately after the movie was over.

Al: "It's a great film, but it made me very sad the way they all turned on Sal. Only Da Mayor (an old man played by Ossie Davis) supports him. Like Sal says, 'These people have grown up on my food.' But they turned on him."

Nick: "This Spike Lee has real talent; they ought to give this thing the Oscar. It really shows it the way it is. It's funny, when I first got into the [restaurant] business, a guy told me, 'Don't trust blacks. If a black guy had a gun and had to choose between killing a white guy he knew and a black guy he didn't know, he'd shoot the white guy.' I don't believe that, but that's what a lot of people think."

Al: "I saw a lot of what we go through in our place in the picture."

Nick: "It's funny about the pictures on the Wall of Fame. If I walked into a black establishment, it wouldn't bother me if there were only pictures of blacks up there. We have a wall, but we cover it with all kinds of people."

Al: "It's Sal's restaurant."

The two men had focused on the destruction of the restaurant but not on the death of the young black man.

Nick: "I'll be honest with you. I completely forgot about that kid dying. This Spike Lee is brilliant. He put so much violence in the destruction of the restaurant that I didn't think about the kid. He died for no reason."

Al: "I'm really embarrassed I didn't think of him. He got it because his friend, Buggin' Out, wanted to be like Martin Luther King Jr. or Malcolm X."

Was that the reason, or did he die because of police brutality?

Al: "The cop got carried away."

Nick: "There were three cops on the kid. They didn't have to kill him. I think the one cop was venting his own anger, his own racism."

Al: "I'm still upset at the way they treated Sal. I was brought up to respect my elders no matter what color they were."

Nick: "This picture throws a lot at you. I'd have to see it two or three more times to get it all. It's as good as 'The Godfather.' But it made me nervous. I knew I was in for trouble as soon as I saw Sal drive up to the restaurant with his Cadillac."

Al: "It's got a lot of characters I've worked with. A lot. We used to have somebody who worked with us who was just like Da Mayor, sweeping up in front, spending the money on liquor. I can't believe how much of our world [Spike Lee] got on film."

Nick: "Even the Italian was good. I mean it, I put this picture in the same class with *The Godfather*. But I don't think it's going to do as much business. I think the white people who see it are going to tell other white people it's a 'black picture.' That would be too bad."

IN A NEW FILM, SPIKE LEE TRIES TO DO THE THING

MICHAEL T. KAUFMAN

Even before *Do the Right Thing* opens on Friday, Spike Lee, its producer, director, writer and star, has already got what he expected most from the film: hot debate, heavy discussion and even denunciation from some who think he did the wrong thing.

The film, both funny and surrealistically sorrowful, has generated torrents of written and spoken commentary. Some who have seen it have warned that it might spark violence. Others have offered tributes, contending that Mr. Lee has dealt with a troubling issue – race relations – in an inspired, honest and troubling way.

The assessments will surely proliferate and clash further once the movie opens. But what is clear enough now is that Mr. Lee, a bold, 32-year-old Brooklyn native, has with this film ventured into an area of film making that has touched a raw nerve.

"Essentially what I hoped was that it would provoke everybody, white and black," said the iconoclastic film maker of the movie, which describes how, on the hottest day of the year, the often amusing foibles, prejudices and conflicting group allegiances of generally symbiotic neighbors in Brooklyn's Bedford-Stuyvesant escalate into a tragic killing of a black man by the police and the torching of a white-owned pizza parlor.

"I wanted to generate discussion about racism because too many people have their head in the sand about racism," Mr. Lee said during a series of interviews conducted by telephone as he shuttled from Los Angeles to Washington, to Atlanta and Houston, promoting the movie. "They feel that the problem was eradicated in the 60's when Lyndon Johnson signed a few documents.

"For many white people, there is a view that black people have the vote and they can live next door to us and it's all done with and there's no more racism. As far as I'm concerned, racism is the most pressing problem in the United States; and I wanted the film to bring the issue into the forefront where it belongs.

"I definitely don't have the answers for racism; but I feel that in order to get to the answers, we have to look at the issues of race and conflict and to say things are not all right. You can hotly debate whether there have really been that many changes in the last 20 years. The black underclass is larger than ever, and it looks like it may be a permanent part of our society."

While the film maker was pleased by all the talk that has preceded the film, he was somewhat angered by articles published around the country suggesting that *Do the Right Thing* might inspire violence. "I knew I would take heat," he said, noting that he had absorbed much criticism, largely from blacks, for his treatment of color prejudices of light- and dark-skinned blacks in his second feature film, *School Daze*. "I figured there would be a hundred times more this time," he said.

"That's O.K. The only thing that really hurts are those articles that are saying that *Do the Right Thing* is going to cause riots. *Do the Right Thing* was not showing the week of the Super Bowl in Liberty City," he said, citing the Miami neighborhood where rioting erupted last winter. "To my knowledge, what happened there was that a cop killed a black kid on a motorcycle who supposedly had robbed someone. That's what started the riot. Better talk about the conditions that make things like that happen. I know black people better than those critics. They are not going to go crazy because of a film. Meanwhile, I know that all you can do is the best you can do, and I did not make this film to make people go crazy."

Mr. Lee, whose film stars Danny Aiello, Ossie Davis, Ruby Dee, Richard Edson, Giancarlo Esposito and John Turturro, as well as the director himself, received very positive reviews in May at the Cannes film festival. But he said that the spate of interviews he has given during the last month has taught him how to take the measure of his interrogators.

"I can tell exactly how white journalists feel about black people by the questions they ask. 'Hey, Spike,' they'll say, 'this Bedford-Stuyvesant looks too clean. Hey, Spike, there's no garbage on the street. Hey, Spike, where are the drugs? Where's the muggers? Hey, I don't see any teen-age women throwing their babies out of windows.' Those were these people's perception of black people in general."

He added that national magazines had done cover stories declaring that drugs were a pervasive problem extending through all sectors of American society. "But do those interviewers ask the people who made *Rain Man* or *Wall Street* why they did not include drugs in their pictures? Those people don't know anything about black people. They've never been to Bed-Stuy. Hell, they've probably never even been across 96th Street."

Mr. Lee himself lives in the Fort Greene section of Brooklyn. He often rides the subway and is a fanatical fan of the New York Knickerbockers. Often critical of those black movie actors and politicians who isolate themselves from more anonymous grit-and-grime blacks, he steeps himself in spontaneously evolving cultural phenomena like rap, line dancing, ornate forms of greeting and sneaker styles. But in terms of his own background, he is very far removed from the ingratiating streetwise con man he plays in his films and in a commercial in which he appears with Michael Jordan.

He grew up in Brooklyn, attending St. Ann's, one of the city's most highly regarded private schools, where his mother taught. His father, Bill Lee, is a jazz bassist who for many years accompanied the singer Odetta.

From the very start of his career, when he was a Wunderkind at New York University's film school, Mr. Lee has taken outspoken positions in defense of black victims of racism. For example, while a student, he attacked professors who, in a discussion of D. W. Griffith's *Birth of a Nation,* neglected to mention that the original showing of the film had been followed by the lynching of hundreds of blacks. After his films gained nationwide distribution, he endowed two programs at N.Y.U. that provided funds to minority students to cover production costs for the movies they made prior to graduation.

The director thinks that none of this will save him from what he anticipates will be criticism from "middle-class blacks," who he assumes will be offended by "what they will regard as negative portrayals of many of the black characters."

Mr. Lee said the idea for *Do the Right Thing* first germinated when he read news accounts of the 1986 incident in Howard Beach, Queens, where white youths attacked three black men, one of whom, Michael Griffith, was killed by a passing car as he sought to escape his tormentors. At the end of the credits for *Do the Right Thing,* Mr. Lee includes a dedication to the family of Mr. Griffith and to the families of five other black New Yorkers who died in controversial circumstances.

Rather than hold himself to the details of the Howard Beach assault, however, Mr. Lee used the incident to stimulate his imagination, for, as he explained, "There's more opportunity in fiction." He has exploited these opportunities in a series of innovative departures. For example, he incorporates music, using the aggressive sounds of rap to mark the pace of looming confrontations. And he splices the narrative flow of his tale with ironic and overblown passages from characters talking to the camera.

There are, nonetheless, several allusions in his film to the Queens assault. For one thing, the central conflict involves blacks and Italians; in one crowd scene, someone refers to Coward Beach; and the Italians use baseball bats threateningly in the film in an echo of what happened the day that Michael Griffith died. As the idea took shape, the first character Mr. Lee sketched out was that of Sal, the hard-working owner of the pizzeria that dominates the street life of the predominantly black area. Sal, played by Danny Aiello, and his two bickering sons are the first white characters Mr. Lee has depicted since his career began soaring with the low-budget *She's Gotta Have It.* Among them, they reflect many complex feelings toward blacks, from polite, perhaps condescending respect, to outright hatred.

"After all, we know more about white culture than whites do about black culture," Mr. Lee said.

Certainly the whites in the film are portrayed as being at least as complex as the array of blacks who dart dramatically through the block, along with some Hispanic neighbors and a Korean grocer. There are people like Buggin' Out, a street hipster who becomes incensed that Sal's Famous Pizzeria's Wall of Fame contains only photographs of Italian show business and sports stars.

There is Radio Raheem, who struts through the streets with a massive boom box, seeking to fill other people's silence with provocative rap music or to drown out other people's noise. There is Mookie, played by Mr. Lee, who delivers pizzas and who tries to reconcile his responsibilities as father, brother, employee, friend and black man as best he can. There are three sidewalk philosophers who comment on the injustice of life and compensate by boasting and teasing one another.

There is also the small but critically important role of Smiley, a simpleminded stutterer who sells copies of a photograph showing the Rev. Dr. Martin Luther King Jr. with Malcolm X. The spirit and thoughts of the two black leaders are brought into play as irritation mounts, forcing most participants to look to their own group and its interests.

At the film's end, Mr. Lee pointedly includes quintessential quotes. First comes one from Dr. King, rejecting violence as evil and ultimately ineffective. That is followed by Malcolm X's assertion that "I don't even call it violence, when it's self-defense. I call it intelligence." It is these final moments that have troubled many viewers, leaving them wondering what Mr. Lee thinks of violence. He explained that dramaturgy had as much to do with his choice of action as any political statement. For example, it had to be Mookie, the character he plays, who escalates the attack on the pizzeria. Until that moment, Mookie has been one of two black characters who has been most sympathetic not only to whites in the film but also, probably, to whites in the audience.

But after the murder of his friend by the police, he, like the community, vents his rage at the only symbol available – the pizzeria where he works. "The audience doesn't expect him to be the one, but that makes the level of frustration real," said Mr. Lee.

In the same way, he said, when the quote from Martin Luther King comes on, he expects the audience, at least the white audience, to have its anxieties assuaged with an appeal to nonviolence. But this, he said, only sets up and underlines the impact of the next quote, the one from Malcolm X. "I did that so that people would think about these issues," Mr. Lee said. The implication of Smiley's hawking of the photo of the two slain leaders, an implication reinforced by the two quotes, seems to be that the lives and beliefs of the two men can somehow be meaningfully synthesized.

"I think they can," said Mr. Lee. "Their lives were certainly inter-twined. I wanted to look at the point where their lives met." He noted that Ossie Davis, the actor who plays Da Mayor, an alcoholic who rises to heroism, had delivered the eulogy at the funeral of Malcolm X. "Ossie told me that at the time of Malcolm X's death, the two men were trying to come together in a common approach that would address issues of economic justice.

"Then, too, there's the reality that it was Malcolm who helped make Martin Luther King more acceptable to white America. Whites could deal with either Malcolm or with Dr. King. Since at the time the Muslims were saying that all white men were dogs or devils, of course they found Dr. King more acceptable than they might have done if Malcolm had not been around."

Mr. Lee said he did not think that either quote precluded the other. "You have to shift tactics," he said.

Whether tactics can indeed override moral imperatives is yet another point of Mr. Lee's film that is likely to fan the debate and discussion he so eagerly seeks.

So, almost certainly, will another segment of the film in which several characters offer what amounts to a fugue of hatred, as each in turn spews forth directly to the film audience his intolerance and hostility for whatever groups he fears and hates.

Mr. Lee was asked whether he believed, as this surreal digression might suggest, that all racism was equally evil.

"I don't think it is," he said. "When somebody spits out some-thing like Jew or Communist, that's obviously not something I can defend or accept, but essentially, bad as it is, it's only name calling. That is very different than the kind of racism that victimizes black people, keeps them from moving forward – racism that kept people from voting or living decently or that gets black people killed."

In the course of transcontinental telephone interviews, Mr. Lee repeatedly emphasized that his major motive in making the film was to stimulate discussion on what he considered to be the major issue facing the country. He added that from a pragmatic perspec-tive, he was pleased that the film would reach the screens as the New York City mayoral race intensified and he hoped that the discussion it generated would help defeat Mayor Edward I. Koch, who, in his estimation, had been significantly responsible for what he said were the deteriorating relations between groups and races. At one point, Mr. Lee explained that he had chosen the title of the film because the phrase resonates with meaning in every group. "Everybody uses it. Italians have that expression. So do blacks." He was asked, in light of the outcry he had provoked, if he ever wondered whether he had done the right thing.

"I'm sure I did," he said. "And I think history will prove that."

Select Bibliography

BOOKS

hooks, bell. *Yearning Race, Gender and Cultural Politics*. Boston: South End Press, 1990.

George, Nelson. *Blackface: Reflections on African-Americans and the Movies*. New York: HarperCollins, 1994.

Lee, Spike. *Five for Five: The Films of Spike Lee*. New York: Stewart, Tabori and Chang, 1991.

Lee, Spike, with Lisa Jones. *Do the Right Thing: A Spike Lee Joint*. New York: Simon & Schuster, 1989.

Tasker, Yvonne. *Spectacular Bodies: Gender, Genre and the Action Cinema*. New York: Routledge, 1994.

Thomas, Laurence Mordekhai. "The Fate of Blacks and Jews." *Vessel of Evil: American Slavery and the Holocaust*. Philadephia: Temple University Press, 1993, pp. 190–205.

Wallace, Michele. *Invisibility Blues*. New York: Verso, 1990.

JOURNAL ARTICLES

Baker, Houston A., Jr. "Spike Lee and the Commerce of Culture." *Black American Literature Forum* 25:2 (Summer 1991): 237–52.

Chrisman, Robert. "What Is the Right Thing? Notes on the Deconstruction of Black Ideology." *Black Scholar* 21:2 (March–April–May 1990): 53–57.

153

Christensen, Jerome. "Spike Lee, Corporate Populist." *Critical Inquiry* 17:3 (Spring 1991): 582–95.

Gates, Henry Louis, Jr. "Final Cut: Spike Lee and Henry Louis Gates, Jr., Rap on Race, Politics, and Black Cinema." *Transition* 52 (1991): 177–204.

Glicksman, Marlaine. "Spike Lee's Bed-Stuy BBQ." *Film Comment* 25:4 (July–August 1989): 12–18.

Hirschman, Elizabeth C. "The Semiotics of Ethnicity: Using Consumption Imagery to Decode Spike Lee's *Do the Right Thing*." *Semiotica* 98:1–2 (1994): 109–37.

Johnson, Victoria E. "Polyphony and Cultural Expression: Interpreting Musical Traditions in *Do the Right Thing*." *Film Quarterly* 47:2 (Summer 1991): 18–29.

Lubiano, Wahneema. "But Compared to What? Reading Realism, Representation and Essentialism in *School Daze, Do the Right Thing,* and Spike Lee's Discourse." *Black American Literature Forum* 25:2 (Summer 1991): 253–82.

Mitchell, W. J. T. "The Violence of Public Art: *Do the Right Thing*." *Critical Inquiry* 16:4 (Summer 1990): 880–99.

"Seeing *Do the Right Thing*." *Critical Inquiry* 17:3 (Spring 1991): 596–608.

Torgovnick, Marianna De Marco. "On Being White, Female, and Born in Bensonhurst." *Partisan Review* 57:3 (1990): 456–66.

MAGAZINE ARTICLES

Ansen, David. "How Hot Is Too Hot? Searing, Nervy and Very Honest." *Newsweek* (July 3, 1989): 65.

"The 'Vision' Thing." *Newsweek* (October 2, 1989): 37.

Biloa, Marie-Roger. "Spike Lee: Un regard." *Jeune Afrique* (June 14, 1989): 60–61.

Canby, Vincent. "Spike Lee Raises the Movies' Black Voice." *New York Times* (May 28, 1989).

"Spike Lee Tackles Racism and Rage." *New York Times* (June 30, 1989).

Carr, Jay. "Spike Lee Spotlights Race Relations." *Boston Globe* (June 25, 1989).

Charen, Mona. "What Is the Right Thing to Do, Spike?" *Newsday* (July 12, 1989): 60.

Corliss, Richard. "Hot Time in Bed-Stuy Tonight." *Time* 134:1 (July 3, 1989): 62.

Dick, Jeff T. "Making *Do the Right Thing*." *Library Journal* 115:9 (May 15, 1990): 106.

Gilliam, Dorothy. "Give Spike Lee a Break." *Washington Post* (July 10, 1989).

Glaberson, William. "One Defendant Is Found Guilty in Racial Slaying in Bensonhurst." *New York Times* (May 18, 1990).

Handleman, David. "Insight to Riot." *Rolling Stone* (July 13, 1989): 104.

Kaufman, Michael T. "In a New Film, Spike Lee Tries to Do the Right Thing." *New York Times* (June 25, 1989).

Kaufmann, Stanley. "A Village in Brooklyn." *New Republic* 201:1 (July 3, 1989): 24–26.

Kempton, Murray. "Spike Lee's Self Contempt." *Washington Post* (August 3, 1989).

Kilpatrick, George. "To Get Respect" (letter to the editor). *New York Times* (May 18, 1990).

Klein, Joe. "Spiked? Dinkins and *Do the Right Thing*." *New York* 22:26 (June 26, 1989): 14.

Kroll, Jack. "How Hot Is Too Hot? The Fuse Has Been Lit." *Newsweek* (July 3, 1989): 64–65.

Lee, Spike. "I Am Not an Anti-Semite." *New York Times* (August 22, 1990).

Logan, Andy. "Around City Hall: Fighting the Power." *New Yorker* (September 11, 1989): 108–17.

McGilligan, Pat, and Rowland, Mark. "If Critics Picked the Oscars." *American Film* 15:7 (April 1990): 26–31.

Nowell-Smith, Geoffrey. "Blackass Talk: *Do the Right Thing*." *Sight and Sound* 58:4 (Autumn 1989): 281.

Orenstein, Peggy. "Spike's Riot." *Mother Jones* 14:7 (September 1989): 32.

Page, Clarence. "Spike Lee's Warning about Race Relations in America." *Chicago Tribune* (June 25, 1989).

Reynolds, Pamela. "Bostonians Review *Do the Right Thing*." *Boston Globe* (July 1, 1989).

Sanoff, Alvin P. "Doing the Controversial Thing." *U.S. News and World Report* 107:2 (July 10, 1989): 51.

Siskel, Gene. "Spike Lee's Mission." *Chicago Tribune* (June 25, 1989).

"This Picture's as Good as 'The Godfather.'" *Chicago Tribune* (June 25, 1989).

Suh, Cindy J. "In a Brooklyn Store, Behind the Cash Register, Looking Out" (letter to the editor). *New York Times* (May 18, 1990).

Tierney, John. "A Few Call Conviction Unfair but Most Reactions Are Muted." *New York Times* (May 18, 1990).

Wall, James M. "*Do the Right Thing*: A Jarring Look at Racism." *Christian Century* 106:24 (August 16, 1989): 739.

Index

Academy Awards, 10, 23, 108
Academy of Motion Picture Arts and Sciences, Best Student Film Award, 3
Adorno, Theodor, 68
aesthetic strategies, 74, 76, 89; in *Malcolm X*, 88–9
aesthetics, in Lee's films, 13, 33, 34, 41, 73–106
African-American community, Lee as mediator between white establishment and, 31–2, 46–7; *see also* black community
African-American culture, 75
African-American filmmakers, 22, 27
African-American music, 53
African-American urban folk cultures, 13, 26
African-Americans, 1, 8; in *DRT*, 11–12, 82; economic exclusion, 40; and ethnic minorities, 36; in film industry, 22; film portrayals of, 17; in film trade unions, 25; in films, 73; mediating expectations of Whites and, 46–7; New York City, 39–40; in U.S. society, 73, 74
Aiello, Danny, 8
alliance politics, 89, 98–9
American flag, 14, 122
antiurban bias, 41, 42, 43
Arrested Development, 52, 88
art, and public taste, 14; *see also* public art
artistic integrity, 17, 20–1
Auge, Marc, 41
aural dialectic, 53, 54
awards, honors, 10, 23

Baker, Anita, 68
Baraka, Amiri, 92
Bedford-Stuyvesant, 8, 11, 19, 26–7, 33–4, 36, 45, 58, 60; as microcosm of African-American culture, 69;

neighborhood characters, 75; racial diversity, 53–4; romanticized vision of, 44
Bender, Thomas, 42
Bensonhurst, 11, 36, 60
Berlin Wall, 13, 126n8
Biko, Steve, 17
black aesthetic, 31
black community, 12, 28, 46; in *DRT*, 34, 35; extended family as, 3–8, 11; political weakness of, 40; and white establishment, 36; *see also* African-American community
black culture, 7, 68, 69
black family, 45
black films, 16; audience for, 74
black history, 51, 52, 70
black identity, 97, 99
Black Muslim(s), 87
black nationalism, 15n7, 40, 75, 77, 85
black performers/artists, 51, 52
black politics, 74, 77, 84; in *DRT*, 98–9; icons of, 80
black politics of identity, 89; *see also* identity politics
black pride, 69, 99, 111
Black United Front, 37
black urban experience, 75; in films, 28
black youth, killing of, 103–4n20
Blacks, *see* African-Americans
Blades, Ruben, 68
Blaxploitation period, 21
blues, 53, 55, 110
Boyz N the Hood (film), 16, 31, 41, 45, 51
Brando, Marlon, 23
Brecht, Bertolt, 75, 76, 87, 89, 93, 96
Brechtian aesthetic strategies, 13, 74, 81, 86, 88, 89, 93, 96, 116
Brechtian morality tale, *DRT* as, 74–8

157